Piano for Pleasure
A Basic Course for Adults

Second Edition

Piano for Pleasure
A Basic Course for Adults

Second Edition

Martha Hilley
The University of Texas at Austin

Lynn Freeman Olson
Composer and Consultant, New York City

West Publishing Company

St. Paul   New York   Los Angeles   San Francisco

Credits

Cover Art: **MATISSE, Henri:** *Memory of Oceania.*
Nice, summer 1952–early 1953.
Gouache and crayon on cut-and-pasted paper
over canvas, 9′4″ × 9′4 7/8″. Collection, The
Museum of Modern Art, New York. Mrs. Simon
Guggenheim Fund. Photograph © 1991 The
Museum of Modern Art, New York.

Cover Design: **Melinda Grosser for** *silk*
Copyediting: **David Severtson**
Composition: **A-R Editions, Inc.**
Music Engraving: **A-R Editions, Inc.**

We wish to thank the many publishers who were so kind to
grant permission to reprint their works. Specific credit lines
appear in the body of the text.

Library of Congress Cataloging-in-Publication Data

Hilley, Martha.
  Piano for pleasure: a basic course for adults /
  Martha Hilley, Lynn Freeman Olson. — 2nd ed.
    p.   cm.

  Includes indexes.
    1. Piano—Methods.   2. Music—Theory, Elementary.
  I. Olson, Lynn Freeman.   II. Title.
  MT222.H63   1992   786.2′ 193—dc20   91-41108
  ISBN 0-314-93369-7   CIP
                                               MN

Dedication

On February 1, 1991, this old world lost one of its better citizens. My brother, Edmond Ray Hilley, died of heart failure at the young age of 49. He was a person who loved music for the sheer joy of it—a man with a wonderful natural gift for music, the making of it and the sharing of it. It is for this reason that I dedicate *Piano for Pleasure* to his memory. May his love of music live on through all of you who use this text.

Publisher's Note

As everyone associated with the world of piano pedagogy well knows, Lynn Freeman Olson, the co-author of this book, succumbed to cancer on November 18, 1987.

Lynn was a most remarkable author. In him dwelt a rare combination of authority and kindness, of professional accomplishment and personal warmth, of undaunting self-discipline and disarming good spirits. Working with him was a stimulating challenge and a happy adventure.

Lynn was a perfectionist who, on behalf of the thousands of students to whom he devoted his life, drove himself to the highest personal and professional standards. He was proud of the books he published with West, and we were—and are—proud to be his publisher.

Contents

1. Listening/Dynamics/Black Keys

2. Simple Note Values/Key Names/Black-Key Groups

3. Meter Signatures/Rests/Line and Space Notes/Steps and Skips/Second and Thirds

4. Recap

5. Treble and Bass/Grand Staff/ Fourths and Fifths/Half Steps and Whole Steps/Sharps and Flats

6. Dotted Rhythms/Phrases

7. Upbeats/Major Pentascales

8. Recap

9. Extension/Triads/Ledger Lines

10. Syncopation/Sixths, Sevenths, Eighths/Major Scales/ Key Signatures

11. Scale Fingering/Primary Chords/Harmonizing/ Transposing

15. Compound Meter/Key Triads

16. Recap

17. Triplets/Primary Chords in Minor

18. Supplementary Repertoire

Preface

Welcome back!

Music certainly should be for pleasure, and where do so many seek musical satisfaction but at the piano? The pleasure is there to be discovered and claimed. The second edition of *Piano for Pleasure* provides one proven way to open these doors.

Music is sound, it is not notes, signs, or terms. We have kept the original format and begin again with **Listening**. We invite you to listen always. What you learn with your ears involved will always be with you. The audio cassette is therefore an integral part of this publication. Find a way to use it in practice whenever the text indicates ( ).

Music can be quite personal. You may not feel immediately at home with every piece or activity you encounter in this book. As fast as pieces go, variety is the spice of repertoire; you should plan to reach out and try, but know that some will simply not be "yours" at once. We know you will enjoy the inclusion of more "familiar" arrangements in this edition.

Regarding activities, they all have the purpose of increasing your knowledge and skill (and thus, your pleasure), so dig in—and be patient with yourself. The moment you participate you are beginning to learn.

Rhythm is an essential musical element, and so we give you some specific practice. The tapping exercises can be performed anywhere; no need to wait for a piano! Relax into a steady beat and feel the rhythms move.

Technique is simply the *way* you achieve sounds, a good technique is an efficient one. Our "Tabletop" exercises do not require a piano, so launch into them whenever and wherever you can.

Theory describes how music is put together—the ways and wherefores as well as terminology—but always brought to the keyboard.

Reading principles and drills provide a way for you to translate the written symbols into sound. Regular practice will allow you to possess this skill.

Improvising within guidelines, "on the spot," brings music to life and helps make its expression most personal. Jump in and try; there is no wrong solution to an improvisation assignment.

Performance is a natural part of musical pleasure. In a very real sense, music cannot live until it is performed. You will play at every step along the way, at each level you reach. Always ask yourself how each piece expresses feelings, moods; explore how the piece is organized.

You will wish to demonstrate the following qualities as you move through these materials with your teacher:

> **Curiosity**—ask "why" and "how"
> **Confidence**—jump in, play the piano, and keep going even if you drop a few sounds along the way
> **Patience**—take the time to let your ears, mind, and muscles learn (they will!)
> **Industry**—in general, you cannot will these skills into being; you must devote some time for workout on a regular basis

The bottom line is always enjoyment—music for the lifelong values of personal achievement, aesthetic awareness, emotional expression, and social interaction.

It's a pleasure to welcome you to the world of music at the piano.

Acknowledgments

When news of a second edition leaked out, there were many pedagogical voices heard saying, "don't fix it, it isn't broken!" Let me assure you that neither Lynn nor I considered *Piano for Pleasure* to be broken, but we did feel that there were things that could be "adjusted", added to and/or taken from.

The audio cassette will remain with this edition; therefore, I wish to once again thank those individuals who gave so freely of their talent; **pianists:** Esther Chung, Denise Chupp, Steve Havens, William Chapman Nyaho, Greg Partain, Jay Surdell, Chuck Vinson and William Wellborn; **The Haydn Jazz Quartet:** Geoff Haydon, Barry McVinney, William McKay and Shaun Smith; **strings:** Cathy Haines, Elliott Cheney, Laurie Stevens and Kerri Lay; **recording engineers:** Bob Roberts and Ray Fishel; **producer, director and narrator:** Dr. Merrill Staton.

I wish to thank those who took the time to respond to my letter requesting suggestions for this edition: Nancy Rice Baker, University of Wisconsin-Eau Claire; Russell Bliss, Nassau Community College; Anna Belle Bognar, Bowling Green State University; Stephen Busch, Colorado State University; Angeline Case-Newport, Memphis State University; Sandy Coryell, Millikin University; Betty Anne Diaz, Columbus College; Anna Farina, University of Central Florida; Joann Feldman, Sonoma State University; Kathy Fehrmann, Kansas Newman College; Helen Galloway (retired), Winona State University; Patricia Halbeck, Austin Peay State University; Gordon P. Howell, Bethel College; Michael Keller, University of Wisconsin-Stevens Point; Frances Larimer, Northwestern University; Jerry E. Lowder, Ohio State University; Madeline Hsu, Boise State University; Claudia McCain, Western Illinois State University; John T. O'Brien, Columbus College; Naomi Oliphant, University of Louisville; Larry Rast, Northern Illinois University; Joan Reist, University of Nebraska-Lincoln; Larry Scully, Valdosta State College; Jerry Smith, Los Medanos College; Joanne Smith, University of Michigan; Rebecca Shockley, University of Minnesota; Paul Stroud, California State University-Long Beach; Tom Wade, Glassboro State College; John Walker, Los Medanos College; Dallas Weekley and Nancy Arganbright, University of Wisconsin-La Crosse; Krista Whaley, Baylor University; Gary Wolf, University of Central Florida; Jeanette Constance Wong, California Baptist College; Shirley Woodward, Modesto Junior College; and very special thanks to T. J. Lymenstull, Doug Ashcraft and Marienne Uszler, University of Southern California as well as Tanya Gille, University of Colorado at Boulder. For any omissions, I do apologize.

Thanks also to West Publishing personnel Clark G. Baxter (acquisition editor), Jayne Lindesmith (production editor) and David Severtson (copy editor), whose dedication to music and editorial expertise produced this second edition; Kathy Morton deserves praise for her assistance with permissions. Special thanks to James Schnars for his timely and attentive work in procuring permissions. And as always, to Lynn and all of the memories I have of our work together, I am forever grateful.

Martha Hilley

Piano for Pleasure

A Basic Course for Adults

Second Edition

2

1.

Listening/Dynamics/Black Keys

LISTENING

1-1

Listen to the recorded examples; determine the "feel" of each. Is there a "feel" for 2s; a "feel" for 3s?

RHYTHM

1-2

1. Listen to the recorded examples. Some are "in 2," some "in 3." Determine the feel and play strong pulses.

Example:

    "in 2":   PLAY (*off*) PLAY (*off*)

    "in 3":   PLAY ___ ___ PLAY ___ ___

When you play, use single black keys with your left hand. Move up and down the keyboard at will.

2. Rewind the Cassette to 1-2. Play with the recorded examples, this time playing strong pulses with your left hand as before but filling in the other pulses with your right hand. Again, use single black keys.

Example:

    "in 2":   PLAY play   PLAY play   PLAY *etc.*
               LH   rh   LH   rh   LH

    "in 3":   PLAY play play   PLAY play play *etc.*
               LH   rh   rh   LH   rh   rh

This is an improvisation, so feel free to explore the full range of the keyboard on any black keys.

TECHNIQUE

In keyboard study, fingers are numbered as follows.

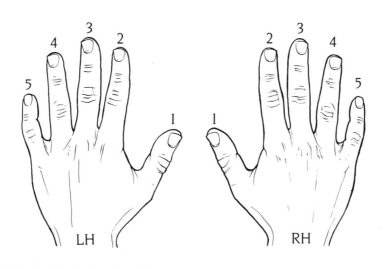

Let your arms hang at your sides. Notice how the fingers are slightly curved at the middle joint. This is a natural, unforced, relaxed hand position. Place both hands on a flat surface in front of you. Maintain the natural shape of your hand. Notice the slightly "rounded" condition of your fingers and overall hand shape; this is the most natural and best position for your hands in playing the piano.

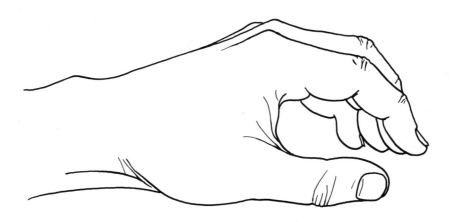

1-3

Follow the directions on the Cassette as you are asked to tap corresponding fingers together.

THEORY

Dynamics are very important elements in any music.

1-4

1. Perform the following exercises with the dynamic level indicated as the Cassette provides a musical background.

LOUD:	Tap	Clap	Tap	Clap	*etc.*		
SOFT:	Tap	Clap	Clap	Tap	Clap	Clap	*etc.*
LOUD:	Tap	Clap	Clap	Clap			
	Tap	Clap	Clap	Clap	*etc.*		

2. Repeat the following pattern eight times starting softly, getting louder, and ending softly.

Tap   Clap   Clap   Clap

Dynamics   Degrees of loudness and softness; intensity.
Forte   Loud (f)
Piano   Soft (p)
Crescendo   To get gradually louder (cresc., or $<$)
Decrescendo   To get gradually softer (decresc. or $>$)

READING

Tabletop Reading   With both hands on a flat surface, play the following exercises with the cassette background (Dash means "hold.")

Exercise 1

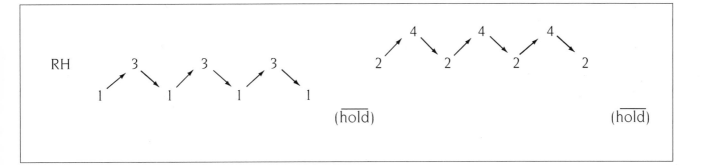

Exercise 2

Exercise 3

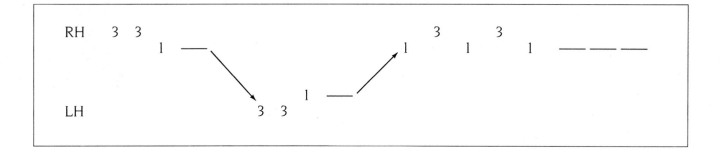

Exercise 4

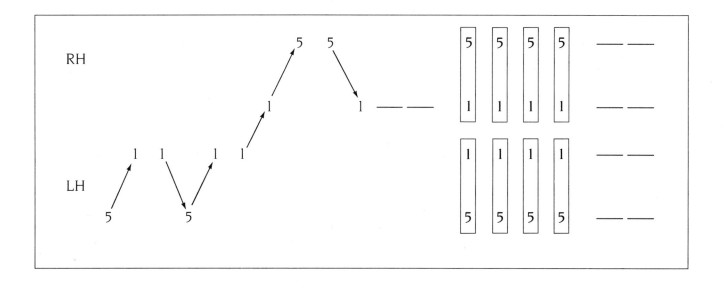

Exercise 5

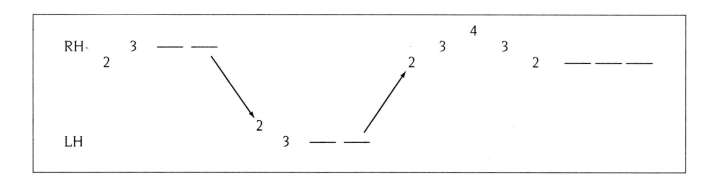

Exercise 6

Exercise 7

IMPROVISING

1. Play single tones on black keys only, alternating between left and right hand while your teacher plays an accompaniment.

There are no wrong notes in improvisation. Feel free to experiment. Listen carefully and follow your teacher's dynamic levels.

Teacher Accompaniment:

p   Continue with varying dynamic levels.

2. Repeat the improvisation and this time experiment with the effect of any of the pedals on your instrument.

PERFORMANCE

1. Your first performance will be based on the rhythms found within a limerick.

Invention on a Limerick

L.F.O.

	X		**X**
There	√ was a young	√ lady named	√ Bright (—)

	X		**X**
Whose	√ speed was far	√ faster than	√ light (—)

	X	
She	√ went out one	√ day

	X	
In a	√ relative	√ way

	X		**X**
And	√ returned home the	√ previous	√ night. (—)

Arthur Buller

Part 1 Solo
Play the rhythm of the words on single black keys. You may use various fingers and keys, but always shift back and forth from hand to hand, changing for each syllable.

Example:

```
          R     R     R           R
There was a young lady named Bright.
     L        L        L     L
```

Part 2 Solo
Play a steady pattern on a group of three black keys to match the √ marks shown. Play in the middle of the keyboard.

Part 3 Group
Play a steady drone pattern, lower on the keyboard. Create the drone by playing these keys simultaneously to match the x marks shown.

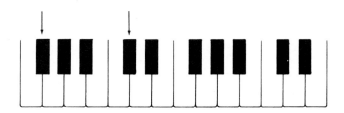

Create a longer piece of music.

a. Part 3 begin the drone.
b. Part 2 enter on the fifth drone sound.
c. Part 1 enter when it feels right.
d. Another solo: Take over Part 1 the second time through the limerick. Use keys higher on the piano.

Theme on a Curve

L.F.O.

2. Practice tapping on a flat surface while saying:

(RH)	TAP	TAP	TAP	-	hold
	TAP	TAP	TAP	-	hold
	TAP	TAP	TAP		TAP
	TAP	TAP	TAP	-	hold

Repeat, using RH finger 2 and a light forearm motion.

Repeat, adding lateral motion while pointing to this keyboard melody chart, touching the indicated black keys.

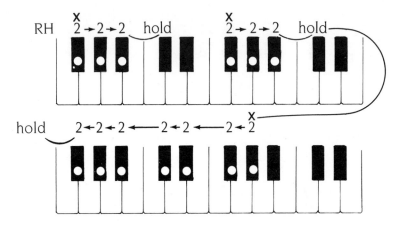

Next, play the same pattern on the piano.

Add a part for LH. Use fingers 5 and 1 on the pair of keys shown, low on the keyboard. Play and hold each time an **X** occurs in the melody chart.

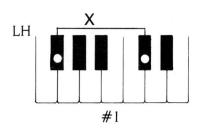

Play again, using another LH pair.

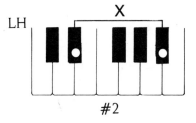

Theme on a Curve involves playing the melody three times, without stopping:

    a. with LH pair #1—*f*
    b. with LH pair #2—*p*
    c. with LH pair #1—*f*

Create your own variation on black keys while keeping the LH as originally played.

3. In the center of the keyboard, find the following black-key groups:

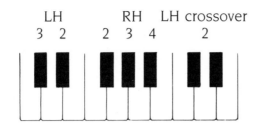

Amazing Grace

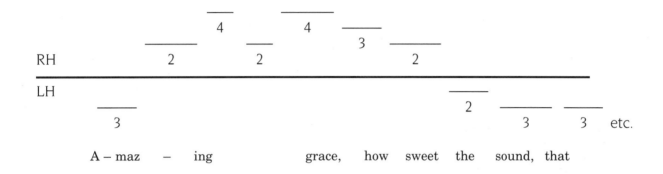

A – maz – ing   grace,   how   sweet   the   sound,   that

Teacher Part

Arranged by M. Hilley

2.

Simple Note Values/Key Names/ Black-Key Groups

LISTENING

2-1

Listen to the rhythms performed on the Cassette and "tap back" after each example.

RHYTHM

♩	= Quarter note
𝅗𝅥	= Half note
♫	= Two eighth notes
𝅝	= Whole note

1. Different note values are used as symbols to illustrate rhythms. It is important to understand the relationship of note durations. For example:

♩ = ♫

𝅗𝅥 = ♩ ♩ = ♫ ♫

(Also written: ♬)

𝅝 = 𝅗𝅥 𝅗𝅥 = ♩ ♩ ♩ ♩

Tie A curved line connecting two adjacent notes of the same pitch. The first note is played and held through the value of the second note.

 sounds same as 𝅗𝅥

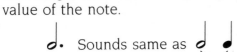 Dotted half note. A dot (·) following a note adds ½ the original value of the note.

Sounds same as

Recorded examples on the Cassette will demonstrate the following rhythms. Listen and tap back as you watch the note values.

2-2

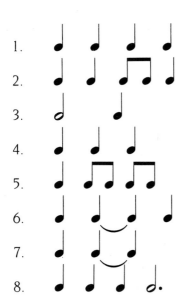

Traditionally, note values are grouped together in equal sets marked off by vertical barlines.

Example:

Stems extending upward are placed to the right of the note head.

Stems extending downward are placed to the left of the note head.

2. Tap the following rhythms on a flat surface. Use these syllables to maintain a steady pulse.

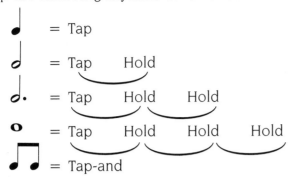

Use RH for upward stemmed notes, LH for downward stemmed notes.

Prepare by saying:

Pulse, Pulse, Ready, Tap

Pulse, Pulse, Ready, Tap

Pulse, Pulse, Ready, Tap

Pulse, Pulse, Pulse, Pulse, Ready, Tap

> **Ostinato** A short pattern of sounds
> repeated continuously.

3. Play each of the preceding rhythm patterns on the keyboard. Use various single black keys
   in each hand. Your teacher will provide an ostinato accompaniment. Before you begin,
   discuss the dynamics to be used.

4. Practice the following rhythm exercises. (When a box shows in place of a word, do not make any sound.)

a. TAP	CLAP	TAP	CLAP
b. TAP	CLAP	☐	CLAP
c. TAP	☐	TAP	CLAP
d. TAP	☐	☐	CLAP

Now perform the rhythm drills with the Cassette as a background. Your teacher will call out the order.

2-3

TECHNIQUE

Tabletop exercises With both hands on a flat surface, play the following examples using the indicated fingering. As a class, determine the speed for each example.

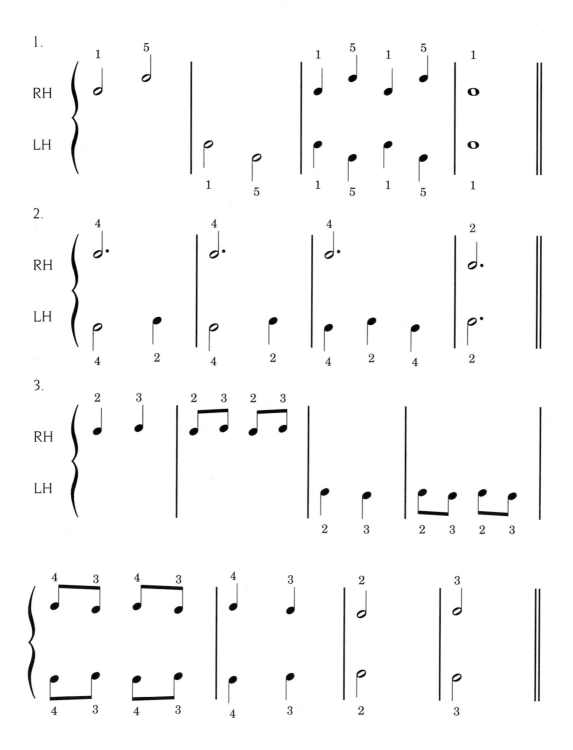

The Music Alphabet Seven letters,
A B C D E F G, which are repeated over
and over for the full range of the
keyboard.

---

1. Starting with the lowest A (to the left) on your keyboard, play from A to the highest key (to the right). Alternate finger 2 in the left and right hands. Use the following keyboard diagram as a guide.

A B C D E F G A B C D E F G A B C *etc.*

With what letter did you end? _____

Practice saying and playing the music alphabet forward and backward. Start with the *lowest* (to the left) A on the keyboard.

→
ABCDEFG—ABCDEFG—
←

Repeat several times on the keyboard starting with a different A each time.

2. The pattern of two and three black keys on the keyboard helps in locating specific white keys. For example, C is to the left of the two black keys; F is to the left of the three black keys.

F C F C F C

3. The following piece has a feeling of 4. Listen to the teacher part, then add the indicated fill-in on the second time through.

Blues for Two

L.F.O.

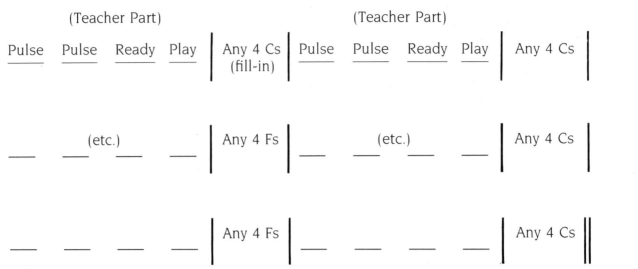

Teacher Part

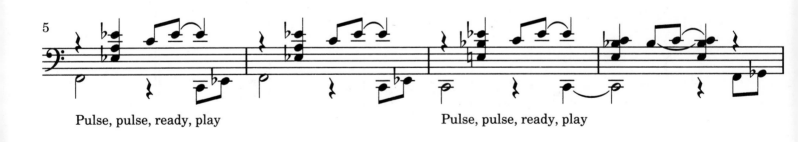

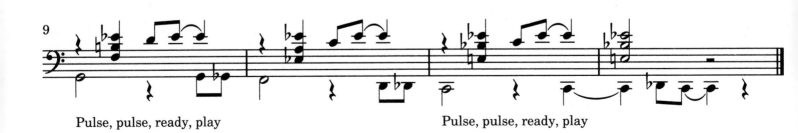

2-4

4. The Cassette will give a letter name. Using the rhythm below, answer with the two letter names that follow each given letter.

For example, you will hear:

Pulse, pulse, begin   A ____ ____

Following A, you would say: "B"   "C"

Begin example 2-4 on the Cassette.

2-5

5. The Cassette will give a letter name. Repeat the exercise as in 4, this time naming the letters backward from each given letter.

For example, following A, you would say "G"   "F".

2-6

6. *Tabletop exercises*   Using a flat surface, practice the following examples as the Cassette provides a background.

a. Pulse, pulse, ready, play

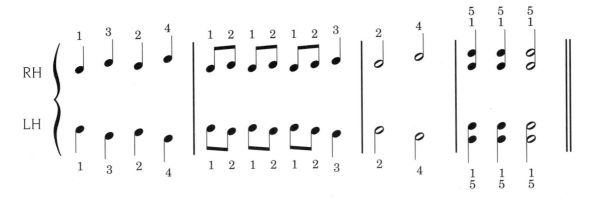

b. Pulse, pulse, pulse, pulse, ready, play

7. Name the final pitch in each pattern. Think the intervening pitches.

Example:

Pulse, pulse, ready, begin:

C (D) (E) (F) | G

Move upward through the pitches.

Pulse, pulse, ready, begin:

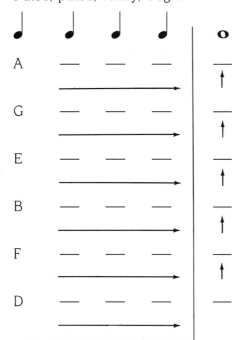

Now play all five pitches of each pattern and name only the starting and ending letters as you play. Use fingers 5 4 3 2 1 of the left hand. Your teacher will provide an accompaniment.

Repeat the patterns with the right hand. Which fingers will you use?

Teacher Accompaniment

mf detached

READING

In the following two pieces, group 1 performs the RH part (part 1); group 2 performs the LH part (part 2). Repeat each piece and switch parts.

Rain

L.F.O.

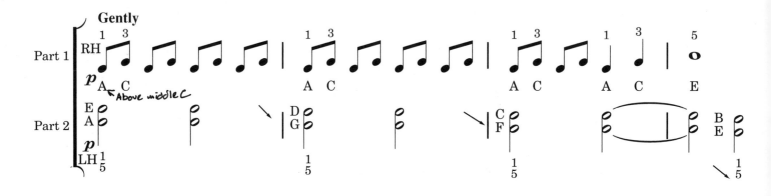

Song for September

L.F.O.

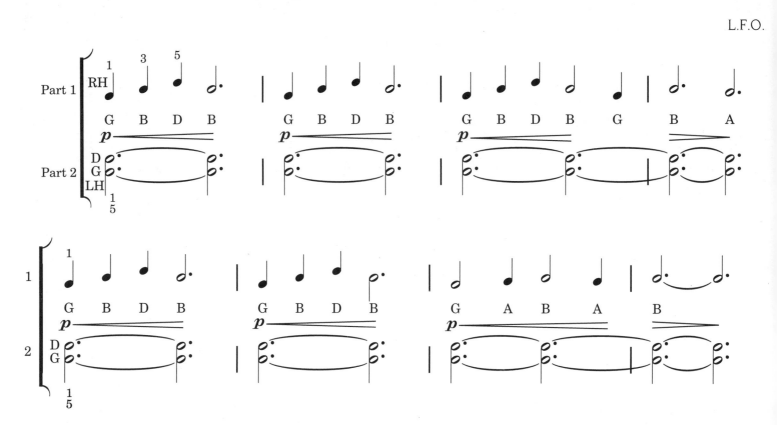

IMPROVISING

1. Use the following keys to improvise as your teacher provides an accompaniment.

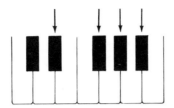

Teacher Accompaniment

2. Use the same pitches as above to play answers to your teacher's musical questions. Remember, these are improvised answers, not echoes. The teacher's score is on the next page.

Moderately

[Student–RH alone]

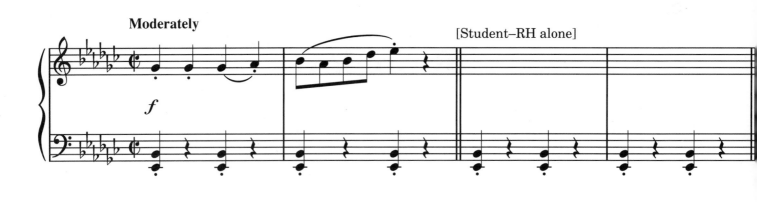

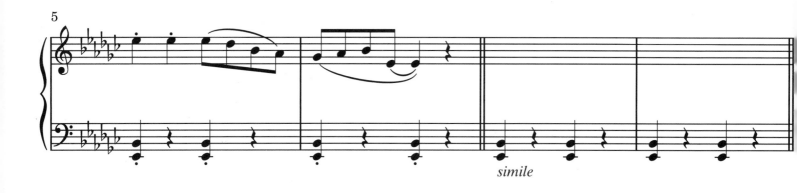

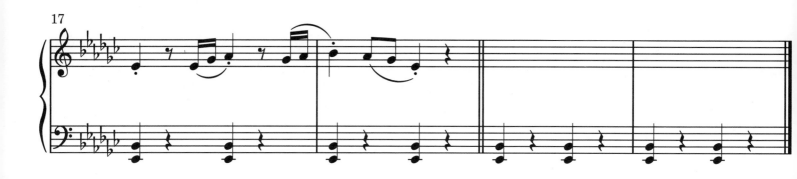

Branches

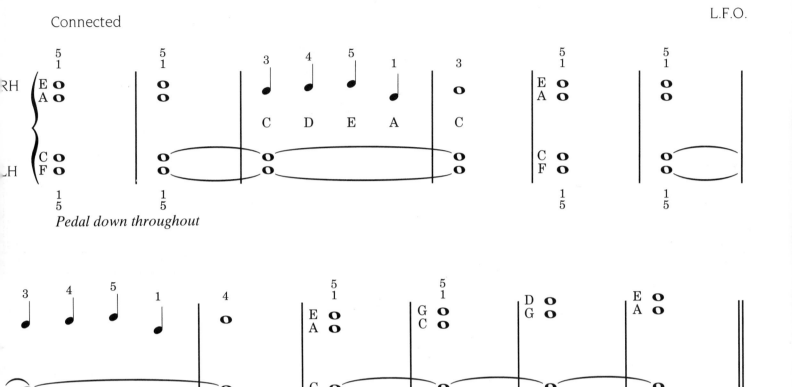

Old School Song

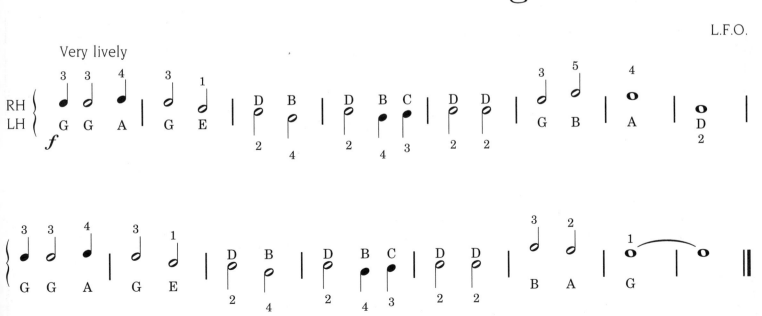

Swing Low, Sweet Chariot

Spiritual
Arranged by M. Hilley

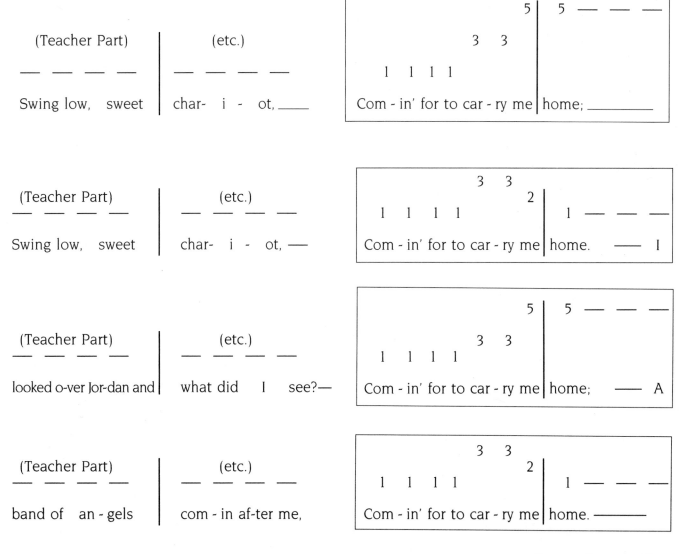

(Teacher Part)	(etc.)	5 5 — — —
— — — —	— — — —	3 3
		1 1 1 1
Swing low, sweet	char- i - ot, ___	Com - in' for to car - ry me home; _____

(Teacher Part)	(etc.)	3 3 2
— — — —	— — — —	1 1 1 1 1 — — —
Swing low, sweet	char- i - ot, —	Com - in' for to car - ry me home. — I

(Teacher Part)	(etc.)	5 5 — — —
— — — —	— — — —	3 3
		1 1 1 1
looked o-ver Jor-dan and	what did I see?—	Com - in' for to car - ry me home; — A

(Teacher Part)	(etc.)	3 3 2
— — — —	— — — —	1 1 1 1 1 — — —
band of an - gels	com - in af-ter me,	Com - in' for to car - ry me home. ———

Repeat first two lines

Teacher Part

Nobody Knows

American

Quietly

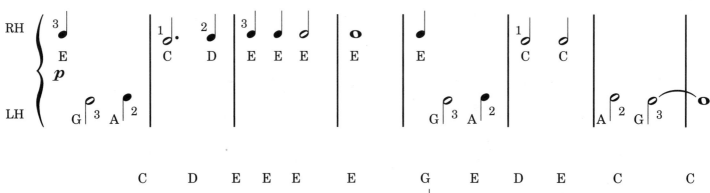

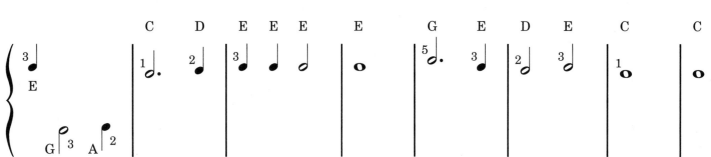

Teacher Chord Chart:

C	F	C	A min
C	F	D min 7	G7
C	F	C	A7
D min 7	G7	F	C

WRITING

1. Copy the following rhythm patterns in the space provided below each. Tap each rhythm after you have copied it.

a.

b.

c.

2. Furnish the missing note values for *Swing Low, Sweet Chariot.*

30

3.

Meter Signatures/Rests/Line and Space Notes/Steps and Skips/ Seconds and Thirds

LISTENING

3-1

1. Listen to the rhythms performed on the Cassette and tap back after each example. Directions will be given before each example.

2. Rewind the Cassette to 3-1 and listen again, this time "playing back" the rhythms on the following pitches:

G   A   B   C   D

Experiment with different orders of these pitches. Alternate hands between exercises.

RHYTHM

1. Meter signatures are used to describe the rhythmic organization of music.

Measure   A set of equal pulses marked off by barlines

Example:

Meter Signature (also called Time Signature) A symbol used to indicate the number of pulses (beats) contained in a measure of music (top number). It also indicates the type of note value that will receive a single pulse (bottom number).

Example: $\frac{2}{4}$—two pulses or beats in each measure. With this meter signature, a quarter note receives one beat.

As a class, discuss the meaning of the following meter signatures:

$$\frac{2}{4} \quad \frac{3}{4} \quad \frac{4}{4} \quad \frac{5}{4} \quad \frac{6}{4} \quad \frac{2}{2}$$

2. To insure steady rhythm, it is best to count aloud. For further security, rhythms should be subdivided based on the smallest note value used.

Example:

Count: 1   2   3   4   1   2   3   4

Count: 1 & 2 & 3 & 4 &   1 & 2 & 3 & 4 &

3. Furnish meter signatures for the following rhythm exercises; then tap as you count aloud. Be certain to subdivide when necessary.

a.

b.

c.

d.

e.

4. In music, silence is as important as sound. Symbols used to indicate silence are called *rests*.

> ❞ Quarter rest (equivalent in duration to the quarter note)
>
> ━ Half rest (equivalent in duration to the half note)
>
> ━ Whole rest (equivalent in duration to the whole note; also equals a whole measure of rest no matter what the meter)

Tap the following as you count aloud.

a.

b.

c.

d.

5. Count aloud as you tap the following rhythms. The Cassette will provide a background.

3-2

a.

b.

c.

TECHNIQUE

3-3 *Tabletop exercises*   Practice the following examples on a flat surface. The Cassette will set the tempo.

1.

2.

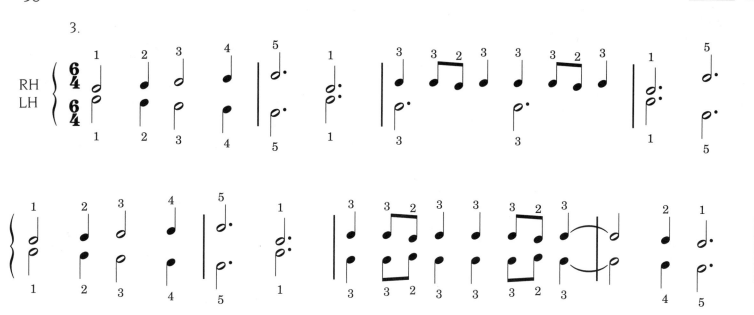

3.

RH
LH

Repeat the last example on the keyboard. Use the indicated beginning pitches and follow the fingering patterns.

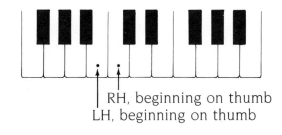

RH, beginning on thumb
LH, beginning on thumb

THEORY

1. The Cassette will call for random pitches to be played on the keyboard. Use a wide range and alternate between the hands.

3-4

Example:

Cassette: 1 2 play an A | 1 2 3 A
                                 student plays ↑

2. The Cassette will give a key name. In rhythm, answer with the TWO pitches that follow, wait a measure, and then play all three pitches.

3-5

Example:

Cassette: 1 2 begin | F "G" "A"
                             ↑   ↑
                            say

           1 2 play | F   G   A
                         ↑   ↑   ↑
                        play

READING

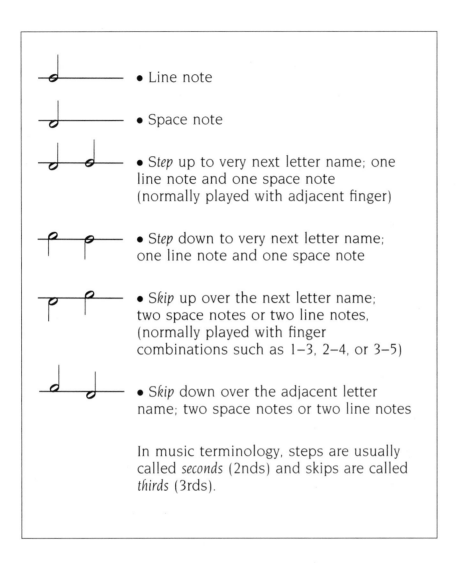

- Line note

- Space note

- *Step* up to very next letter name; one line note and one space note (normally played with adjacent finger)

- *Step* down to very next letter name; one line note and one space note

- *Skip* up over the next letter name; two space notes or two line notes, (normally played with finger combinations such as 1–3, 2–4, or 3–5)

- *Skip* down over the adjacent letter name; two space notes or two line notes

In music terminology, steps are usually called *seconds* (2nds) and skips are called *thirds* (3rds).

1. Note heads in music are placed either on a line or in the space above or below the line. The arrangement of notes as line or space notes determines the direction you will move on the keyboard.

Examples:

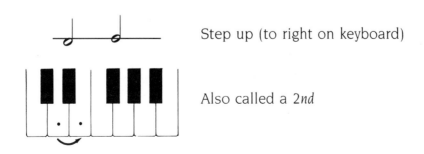

Step up (to right on keyboard)

Also called a *2nd*

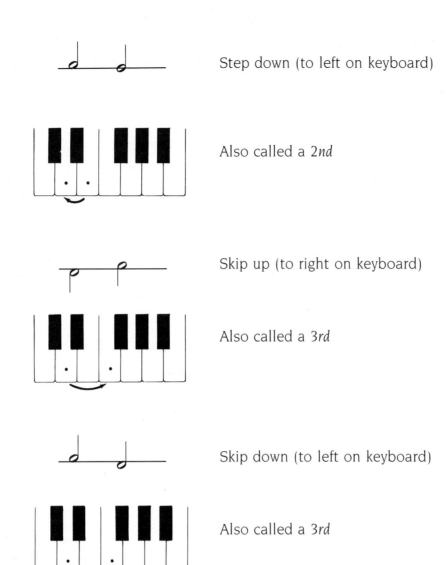

Step down (to left on keyboard)

Also called a *2nd*

Skip up (to right on keyboard)

Also called a *3rd*

Skip down (to left on keyboard)

Also called a *3rd*

Practice playing the following examples of skips and steps (seconds and thirds) on the keyboard.

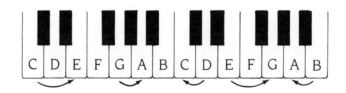

2. Logical fingering is one of the most important components in reading piano music. Stepwise motion in music usually calls for consecutive fingering (1, 2, 3), whereas skips, or thirds, call for a skip in fingering (2–4, 3–5, 1–3).

Discuss possible fingerings for the following examples and play. Count aloud to insure a steady pulse.

a. Begin on E

b. Begin on A

c. Begin on G

d. Begin on F

e. Begin on C

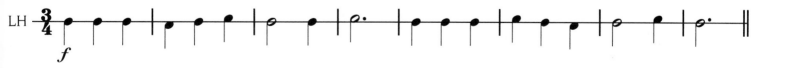

f.   Begin on G

g.   Begin on F

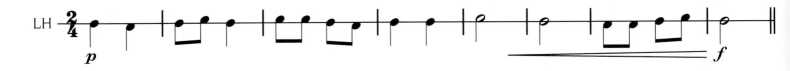

h.   Begin on B

3. Carefully study the following examples.

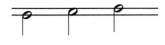 • Step up (to the right on the keyboard)

 • Step down (to the left on the keyboard)

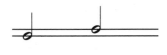 • Skip up (to the right on the keyboard)

 • Skip down (to the left on the keyboard)

4. Determine a logical fingering and play.

a.   Begin on F

b.   Begin on E

c.   Begin on F

Interval   The distance from one key (or note) to another

3. From D to F is an interval of a third. It spans three letter names.

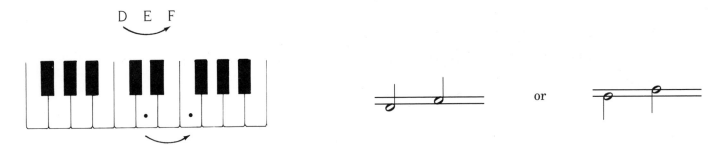

From D to E is an interval of a second. It spans two letter names.

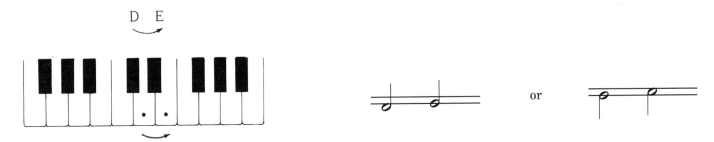

From G to E is an interval of a third. It spans three letter names.

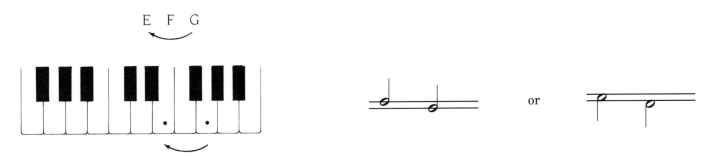

From D to C is an interval of a second. It spans two letter names.

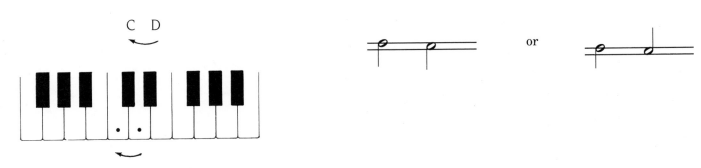

4. Use the music alphabet as a reference.

- Begin with the lowest A and say letter names up in thirds.
- Begin with the lowest B and say letter names up in thirds.
- Begin with the highest C and say letter names down in thirds.
- Begin with the highest B and say letter names down in thirds.

Now go back and play the above exercises. Use alternating hands, finger 2 in each hand.

5. Play through the following interval chains:

- RH Position: D E F G A

    Play: D
        up a third
        down a second
        up a second
        down a third   You ended on_____

- LH Position: D E F G A

    Play: D
        up a third
        down a second
        up a third
        up a second
        down a third   You ended on_____

- RH Position: G A B C D
   Your teacher will dictate intervals.

- LH Position: G A B C D
   Your teacher will dictate intervals.

IMPROVISING

1. Improvise by repeating this two-measure rhythm. Use the five white keys indicated. Your
teacher will provide an accompaniment.

Teacher Accompaniment

etc.

PERFORMANCE

Stomp Dance

Begin on F

Firmly

L.F.O.

Teacher Accompaniment

M. HILLEY

Wind Song

Begin on E

L.F.O.

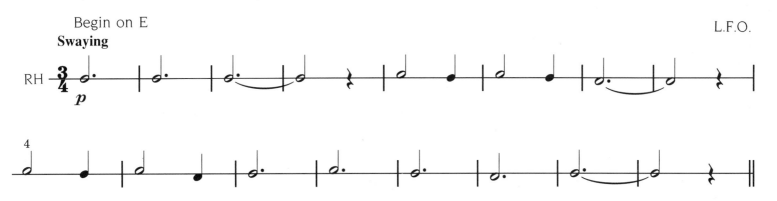

Teacher Accompaniment

M. HILLEY

Catfish

Begin on G

Lively

American

Teacher Accompaniment

M. HILLEY

Round Dance

Begin on D

L.F.O.

Lively

Teacher Accompaniment

M. HILLEY

Lullaby

Begin on E

L.F.O.

Easily

Teacher Part Optional

M. HILLEY

Play through *Romantic Melody* twice.

Romantic Melody

L.F.O.

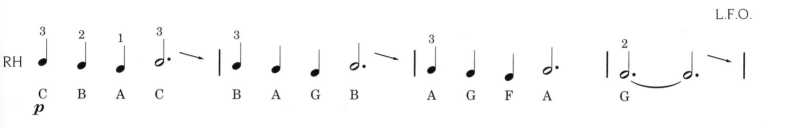

RH

C B A C   B A G B   A G F A   G

p

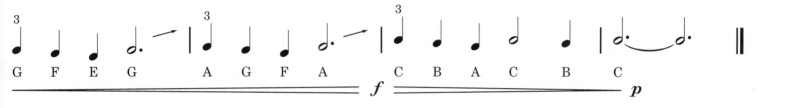

G F E G   A G F A   C B A C B   C

f   *p*

Teacher Accompaniment

p

with pedal

Bim Bom

Arranged by M. Hilley

WRITING

1. Copy the following "directional" rhythms in the space allowed. After copying, tap each rhythm as you count aloud. Determine a logical fingering; then play on the keyboard. Your teacher will suggest the starting pitches.

4.

Recap

PERFORMANCE

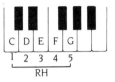

Evening Song

L.F.O.

Teacher Accompaniment

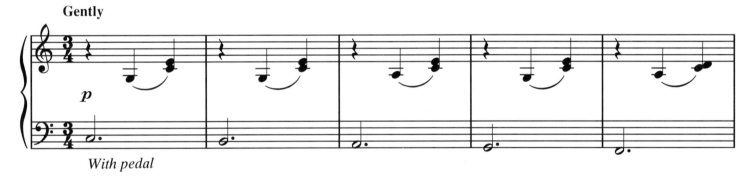

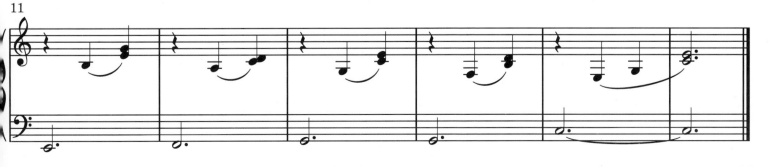

Morning Has Broken

Arranged by M. Hilley

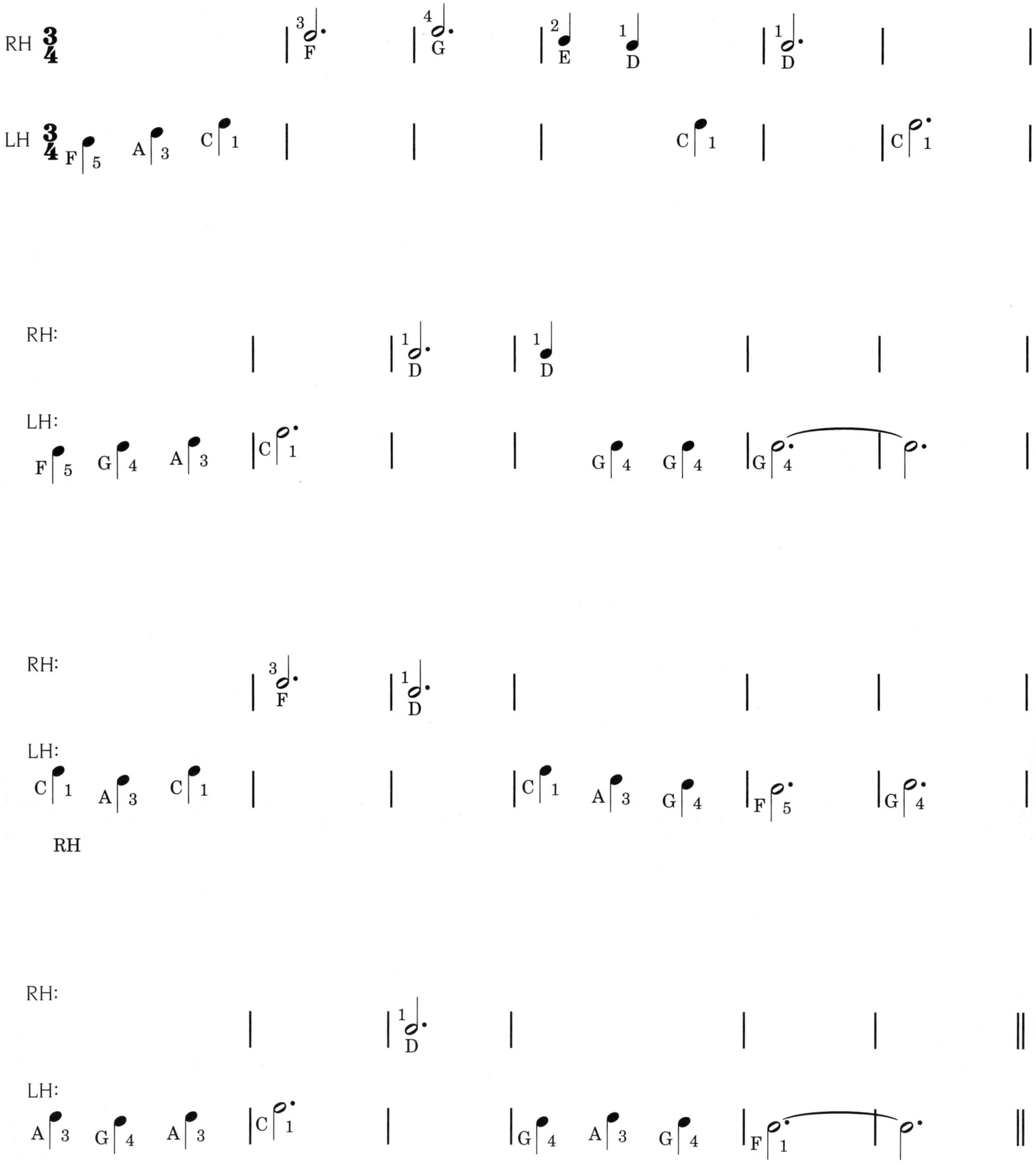

Morning Has Broken

Teacher Accompaniment

Arranged by M. Hilley

Barcarolle

JACQUES OFFENBACH
Arranged by L.F.O.

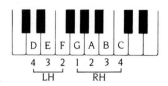

Teacher Accompaniment

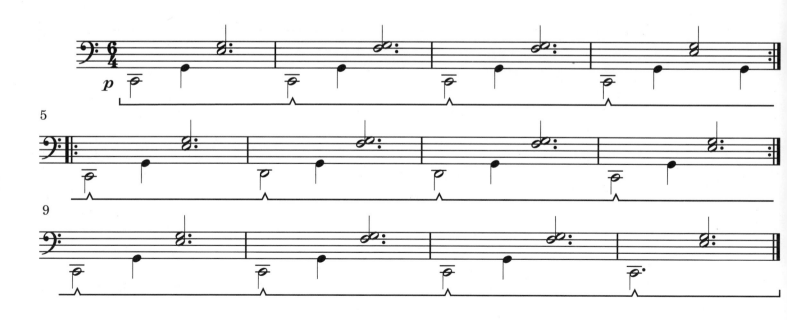

TERMINOLOGY REVIEW

Discuss the following musical terms

- Music alphabet
- Line note/space note
- Step/skip
- Dynamics
- Note values/rest values
- Meter signatures
- Measure/barline
- Stem direction
- Tie
- Ostinato
- Intervals

WRITING REVIEW

1. Add barlines to the following rhythm examples.

4

2. Circle the ONE INCORRECT measure in each of the following examples.

a.

b.

c.

d.

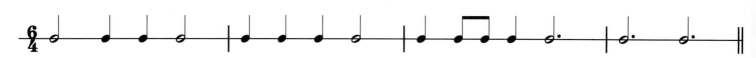

3. Finish this melody any way you like; then play.

Begin on C

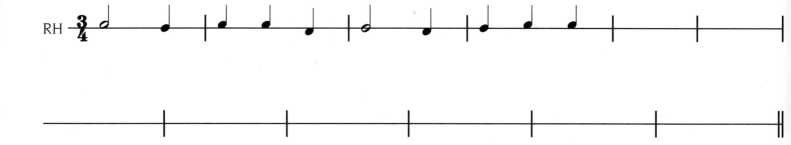

5.

Treble and Bass/Grand Staff/ Fourths and Fifths/Half Steps and Whole Steps/Sharps and Flats

LISTENING

1. Your teacher will play five-tone melodies that move up (➚), move down (➘), remain the same (➝), or use a combination of these motions. Find the picture that matches each melody.

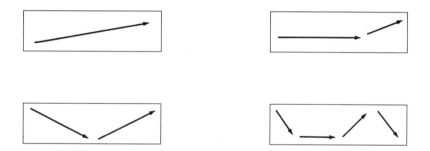

2. Your teacher will play from the following patterns. After hearing each pattern, you will imitate it. Close your book and listen carefully for instructions.

Teacher announces, "Begin RH finger 3 on C. Listen."

Teacher announces, "Begin LH finger 1 on D. Listen."

Teacher announces, "Begin RH finger 2 on D. Listen."

Teacher announces, "Begin LH finger 3 on F. Listen."

RHYTHM

1. Tap and count the following rhythms that use ties.

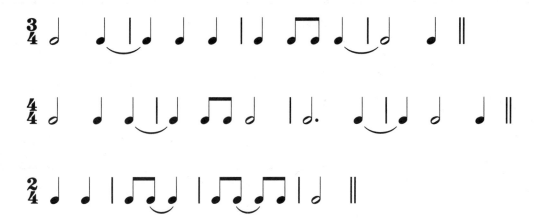

2. Discuss the dynamic levels before performing *Tap It Out.*

Tap It Out

Lively

L.F.O.

Part 1 on metal

Part 2 on wood

Part 3 on leg

Part 4 pair of pencils

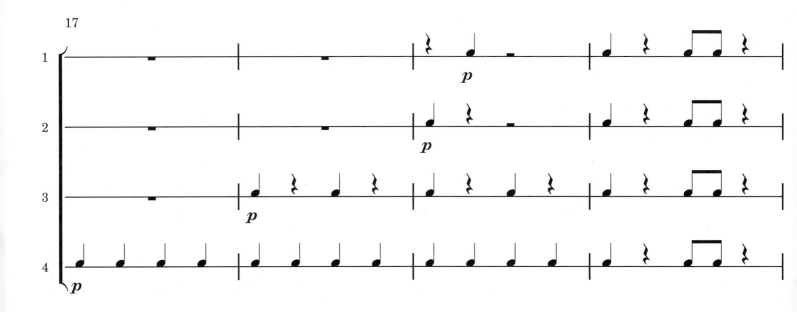

TECHNIQUE

Repeat Sign Return to the beginning and play again, or return to the previous repeat sign and play again.

1. Play the following accompaniment as your teacher provides a melody.

Student Accompaniment

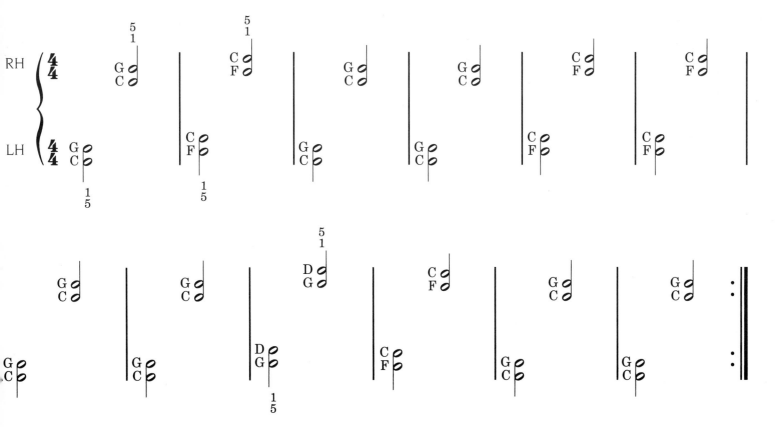

Teacher Melody

THEORY

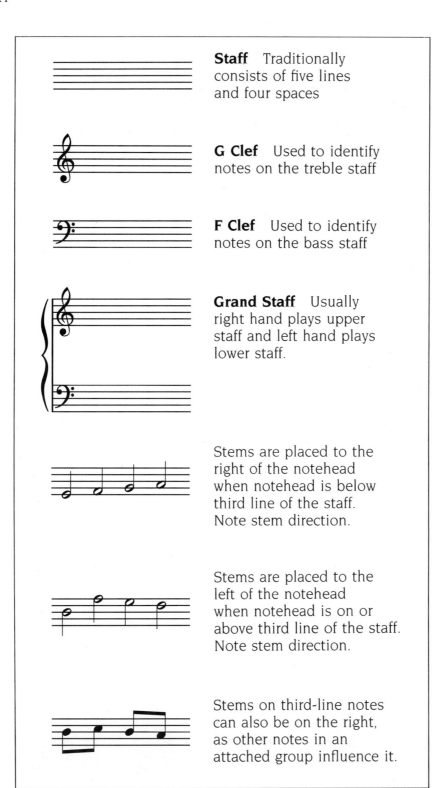

Staff   Traditionally consists of five lines and four spaces

G Clef   Used to identify notes on the treble staff

F Clef   Used to identify notes on the bass staff

Grand Staff   Usually right hand plays upper staff and left hand plays lower staff.

Stems are placed to the right of the notehead when notehead is below third line of the staff. Note stem direction.

Stems are placed to the left of the notehead when notehead is on or above third line of the staff. Note stem direction.

Stems on third-line notes can also be on the right, as other notes in an attached group influence it.

Relationship of Piano Keyboard to Grand Staff

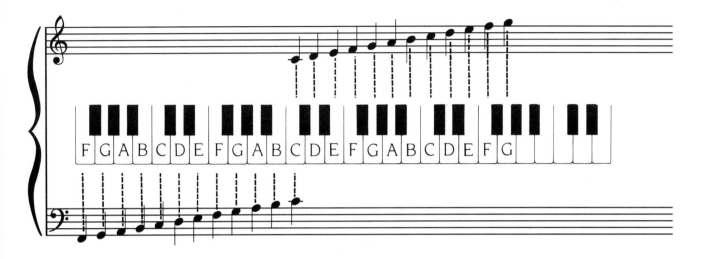

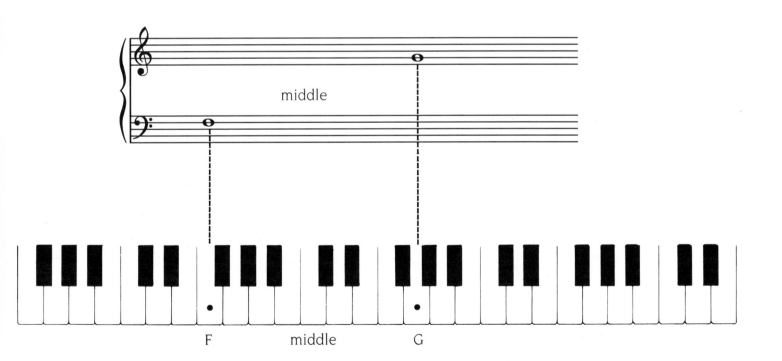

1. Name the first and last note in each measure.

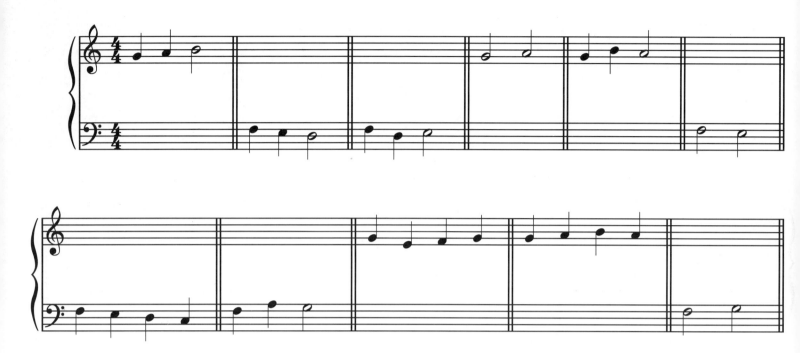

In each measure, select an appropriate beginning finger and play. Name the notes as you play. Notice intervals of seconds and thirds.

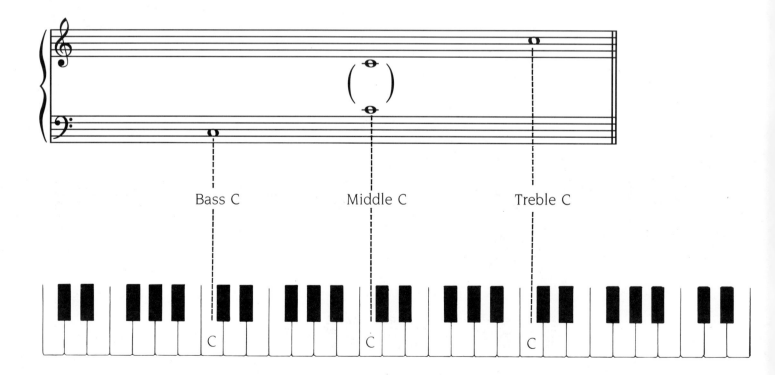

Bass C   Middle C   Treble C

2. Name the first and last note in each measure.

For each measure, select an appropriate beginning finger and play. Name the notes as you play. At each double bar, you may wish to take time to determine the next position.

3. From C to G is an interval of a fifth.

CDEFG

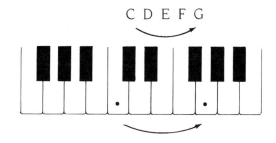 or

From C to F is an interval of a fourth.

CDEF

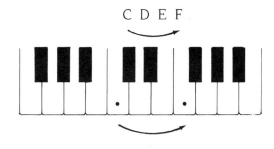 or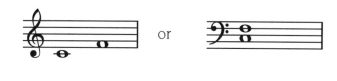

Use the music alphabet as a reference.
- Begin with the lowest A and say letter names up in fifths.
- Begin with the lowest B and say letter names up in fifths.
- Begin with the highest C and say letter names down in fourths.
- Begin with the highest B and say letter names down in fourths.

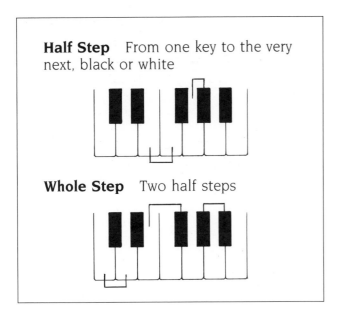

Half Step From one key to the very next, black or white

Whole Step Two half steps

4. On the keyboard provided, mark the half steps that occur from white key to white key.

Play these half steps on your keyboard. They are called "natural" half steps.

♯ **Sharp** Raises a note one half step

♭ **Flat** Lowers a note one half step

The effect of a sharp or flat lasts through the measure.

5. Play the sharp for each given key.

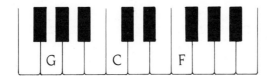

6. Play the flat for each given key.

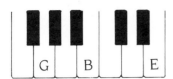 

♮ **Natural**   This sign cancels the effect of a sharp or a flat

---

7. Play the natural key and then the sharp key as shown.

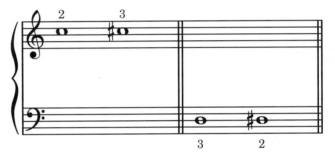

8. Play the sharp key and then the natural key as shown.

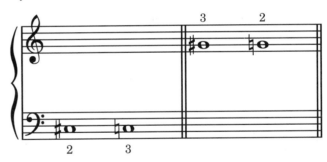

9. Play the natural key and then the flat key.

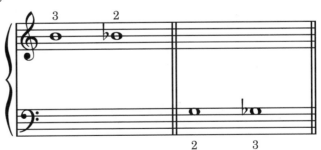

10. Play the flat key and then the natural key.

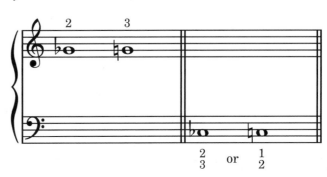

READING

1. Play these interval studies.

2. Look carefully at the following two-measure examples. Your teacher will announce the order in which they are to be played; reading will be nonstop from one to the next.

Position

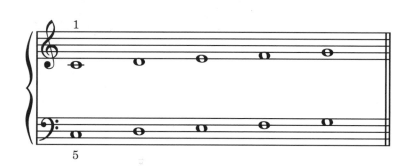

Slur A curved line above or below a group of notes to indicate that they are to be played in a connected manner

3. Play the following revision of *Romantic Melody* as your teacher accompanies. Pay particular attention to slurs.

Romantic Melody Revisited

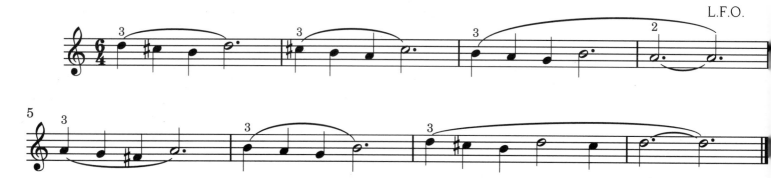

Teacher Accompaniment

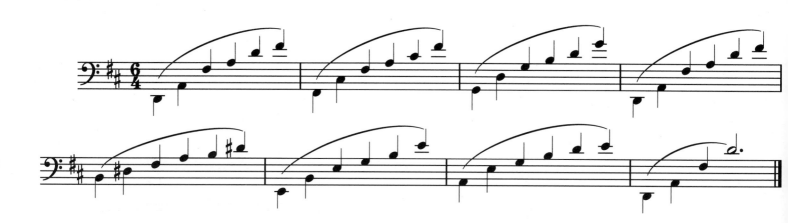

IMPROVISING

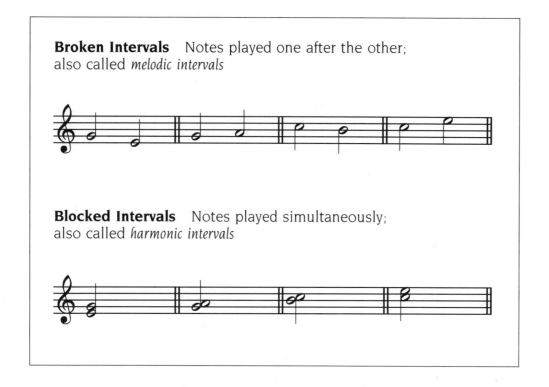

Broken Intervals   Notes played one after the other; also called *melodic intervals*

Blocked Intervals   Notes played simultaneously; also called *harmonic intervals*

1. Play the following broken intervals (melodic intervals).

2. Play the following blocked intervals (harmonic intervals).

3. In a $\frac{4}{4}$ meter, improvise four-measure answers to your teacher's questions. Before beginning each example, establish a keyboard position the same as your teacher's.

Melodic intervals

Harmonic intervals

Your choice

m f	*Mezzo forte*	Medium loud
m p	*Mezzo piano*	Medium soft
>	**Accent**	Sudden strong emphasis

PERFORMANCE

1. This popular folk tune uses both melodic and harmonic intervals.

Clap-Hands Dance

Mexican
Arranged by L.F.O.

2. The melody is divided between left and right hands. Determine the range of each before playing.

Nettleton

American Folk Tune
Arranged by M. Hilley

Teacher Accompaniment

3. What harmonic intervals are used in *To Brahms*?

To Brahms

L.F.O.

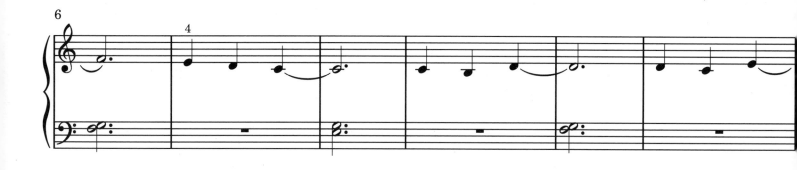

WRITING

1. Use the blank score below to transcribe all parts of *Bim Bom* (p. 48). Perform the ensemble using your score.

Bim Bom

2. Copy the following grand staff examples and then play each from your manuscript.

80

6.

Dotted Rhythms/Phrases

LISTENING

6-1

1. You will hear four musical examples on the Cassette. Listen carefully and identify each example from the music shown below.

6

GEORGE M. COHAN
(1878–1942)

Phrase Musical "sentence" that may or may not be indicated by a curved line. Phrases may vary in length.

2. Listen to the four musical examples again. As a class, determine the phrase lengths in each. Mark the phrases in the music.

Andante Moderately walking

Allegro Bright, moderately fast

Lento Quite slow

Vivace Lively, very fast

6-2
3. Listen carefully to the four musical examples on the Cassette. On a replay, determine which piece is an example of *andante*, which is *allegro*, which is *lento*, and which is *vivace*.

RHYTHM

1. Tap and count the following rhythm examples.

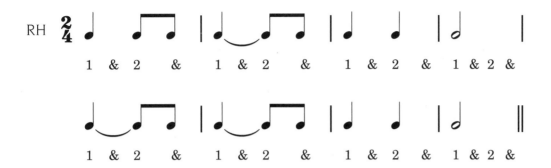

RH

1 & 2 & 1 & 2 & 1 & 2 & 1 & 2 &

1 & 2 & 1 & 2 & 1 & 2 & 1 & 2 &

 Equal in duration to

1 & 2 & 1 & 2 & 1 & 2 & 1 & 2 &

1 & 2 & 1 & 2 & 1 & 2 & 1 & 2 &

6

TECHNIQUE

1. *Tabletop technique*   Practice the following exercises on a flat surface. The Cassette will set
the tempo. Count aloud.

a.

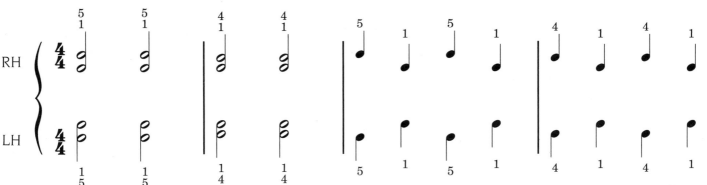

b.

c.

2. Name the beginning pitches of each example. Determine fingering and play.

a.

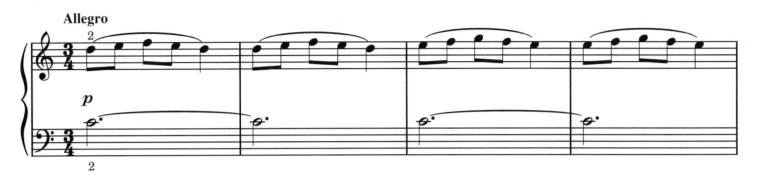

b.

c.

THEORY

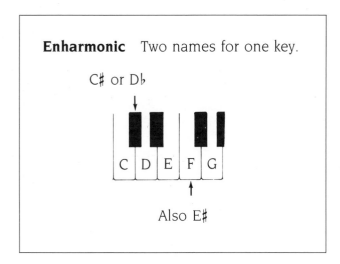

Enharmonic   Two names for one key.

C# or Db

Also E#

Play the sharp key for each given key; then repeat, playing the flat key for each given key.

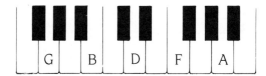

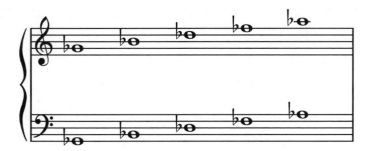

READING

1. *Reading flashes*   Look carefully at the following examples. Your teacher will announce the order in which they are to be played. There will be four pulses of silence for you to prepare each successive example.

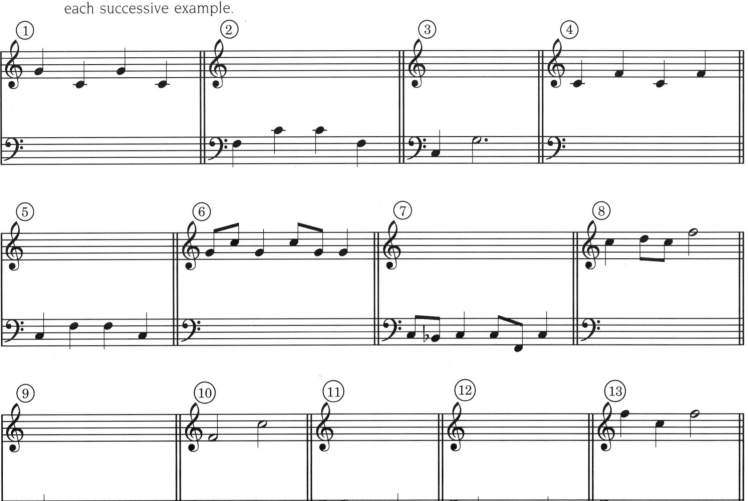

2. Determine fingering and play.

Shifting Light

L.F.O.

3. Name the following notes. Proceed steadily, feeling four beats to a note. Think treble clef.

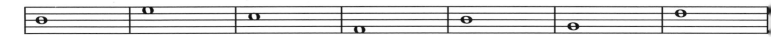

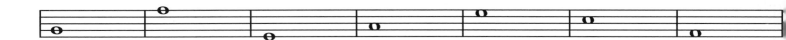

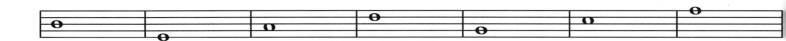

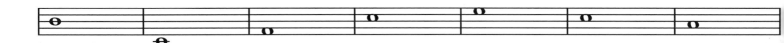

4. Name the same notes again, this time allowing only two beats per note. If you have no trouble doing this, turn your book upside down and do it once again. Think treble clef the first time and bass clef on the repeat.

5. Return to the notes in item 3. PLAY each note, four beats to a note. This time think bass clef. Place a mark by the notes on which you hesitated. Practice the ones that you marked.

Play again, this time thinking treble clef. Place a mark by the ones you hesitated on and practice those again.

If you have no trouble with four beats to a note, repeat the exercise using two beats for each note.

6. Follow the same steps as in items 3 and 5.

IMPROVISING

1. Add all-black-key melodic improvisations above the following black-key ostinato patterns.

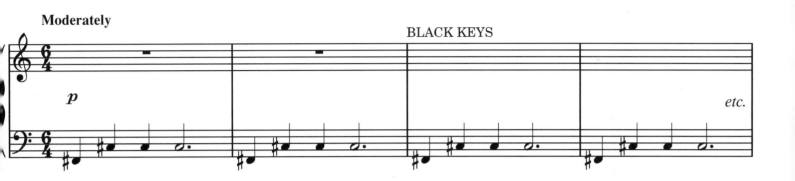

Now improvise your own black-key ostinato with melody.

2. Improvise a piece with three sections.

Section A: Use whole steps that are entirely on black keys; use pedal; involve various rhythms.

Section B: Use whole steps that are white to black or black to white; do not use pedal; involve various dynamics.

Section A: (return)

PERFORMANCE

1. Pay careful attention to dynamic markings.

Miniature March

L.F.O.

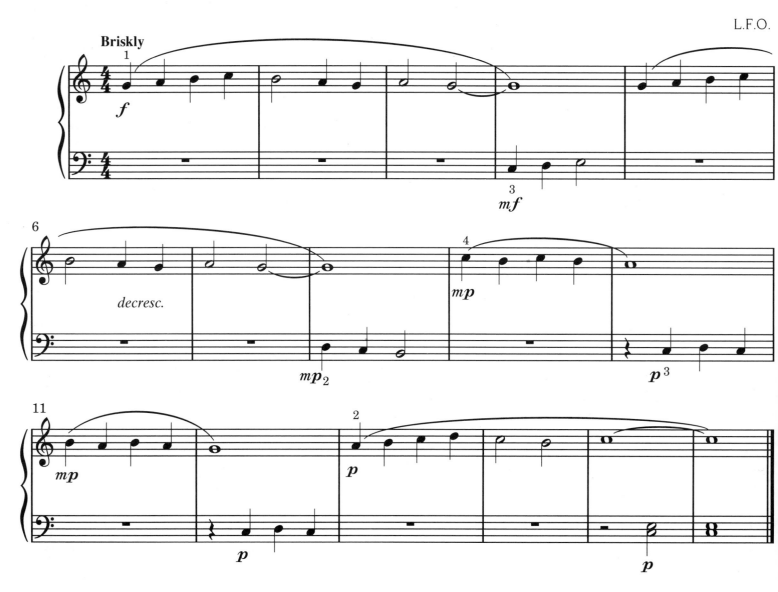

Teacher Accompaniment

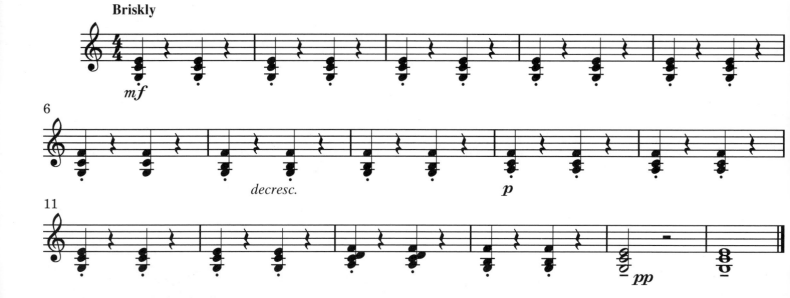

2. Play the C♯ with LH, finger 2.

Pat-a-Pan

Arranged by M. Hilley

3. Note that finger 3 in each hand will always fall on B♭.

A Little Sad

L.F.O.

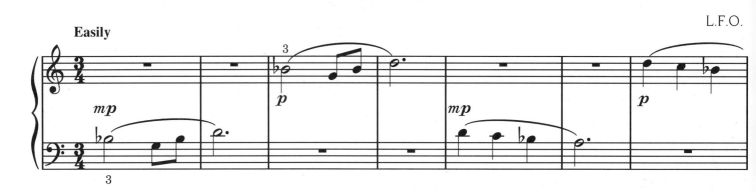

4. Mark phrases as your teacher plays; then perform.

Down in the Valley

American

5. Use consecutive fingering for a connected left hand.

Danza

L.F.O.

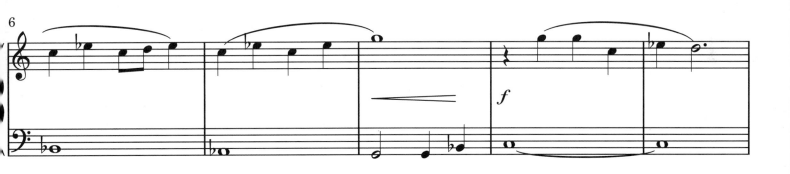

WRITING

1. Study the rhythm "shorthand" illustrated below.

Note	Shorthand	Drawn in Pulse Strokes	
♩	/		One stroke
♩	∟		Two strokes
♩.	∟/		Three strokes
o	▱		Four strokes
♫	⁊		Two quick strokes within one pulse

6-4

Several rhythm examples are played on the Cassette. Write each example using rhythmic shorthand in the space provided. Then convert each example to traditional notes. You will hear each example three times. Example 1 has been written in both rhythmic shorthand and traditional notation to show you how.

a.

b.

$\frac{5}{4}$ | | | ‖

| | | ‖

c.

$\frac{4}{4}$ | | | ‖

| | | ‖

d.

$\frac{3}{4}$ | | | |

| | | ‖

| | | |

| | | ‖

96

Upbeats/Major Pentascales

LISTENING

1. Study the following musical excerpts carefully. Notice that Chopin uses two phrases, which are marked. In Türk's *Allegro non Tanto*, the phrases are not marked. Listen as your teacher plays each excerpt. Identify where the first phrase ends in the Türk.

Prélude

FRÉDÉRIC CHOPIN, Op. 28, No. 6
(1810–1849)

Allegro non Tanto

DANIEL GOTTLOB TÜRK
(1756–1813)

2. You will hear several examples that include fourths and fifths. Close your book and listen as your teacher gives instructions for the playbacks.

RHYTHM

> **Upbeat**   One or more sounds preceding a downbeat (beginning of a measure). The last measure is usually shortened as a result.

1. Tap and count the following rhythm examples that begin with upbeats.

1   2   3 | 1   2   3

& 2 & | 1 & 2 &

2. In the $\frac{4}{4}$ rhythm chart, use the following physical motions for given note values:

 — CLAP

   ♩ — SNAP

   𝅗𝅥 — TAP

Count aloud as you perform only the quarter notes.

Count aloud as you perform only the half notes.

Count aloud as you perform only the eighth notes.

Form a rhythm ensemble by assigning certain note values to certain students. When you perform together, you will hear all the rhythms given.

TECHNIQUE

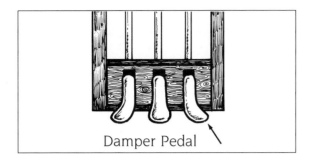

Damper Pedal

1. The following graphic shows the use of the pedal that sustains sounds (a "damper pedal" on acoustic pianos). It indicates foot action. Pedal with heel on the floor; lower and raise the pedal with the ball of the foot. Use right foot.

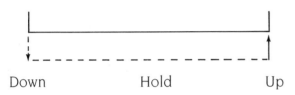

Down   Hold   Up

The graphic below shows connection of sounds. When the key or keys go down, the foot allows the pedal to rise to clear the previous sound and then lowers to catch the new sound. A seamless effect results.

With finger 2, play the following and connect one tone to the next with pedal as shown.

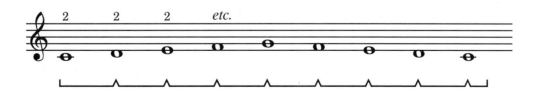

2. Play the following pedal exercises.

a.

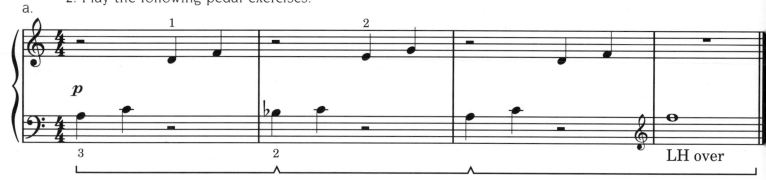

b.

c.

Staccato   Shortened sound
Legato   Connected sound

---

3. The Italian word *staccato* derives from a word meaning to "pull apart" or detach. In playing *staccato*, you do not punch the keys nor jump away from them; you simply shorten each sound by releasing the key. You will feel your hand "release" easily. A dot above or below the notehead indicates *staccato*.

Play each example.

In playing *legato*, note durations are held for full value, resulting in continuous but not overlapping sound.

A special sign is not always necessary to show a legato sound.

4. Determine the range of each example to help in choice of fingering, then play.

a.

b.

c. **Andante**

d. **Andante**

e. **Sturdily**

f. **Lively**

THEORY

Scale   Individual pitches arranged in consecutive order

Pentascale   Five-tone scale using consecutive letter names

---

1. Beginning with RH finger 1, play an all-white-key pentascale starting on G.

There are five pitches—1, 2, 3, 4, 5. The only half step occurs between which pitch numbers?

This is a MAJOR pentascale.

Major Pentascale   Uses the following pattern of whole steps and a half step.

Play and name major pentascales starting on C, D, E, F, G, and A, first RH and then LH. Which of these major pentascales uses a *flat*?

READING

1. *Reading flashes*   Prepare the position shown. During each measure of rest, your teacher will call the number of the next flash to be played. Reading will be nonstop from one to the other.

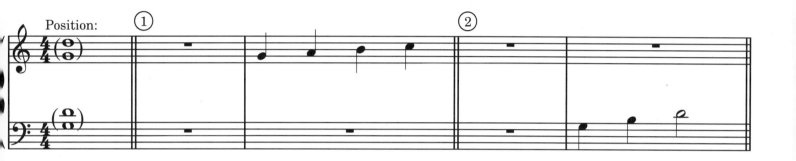

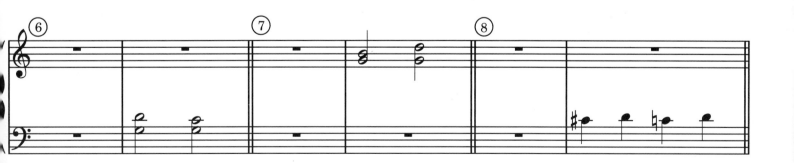

2. During the measure of rest, study each pair of notes; then play hands together. Keep a steady pulse throughout the exercise.

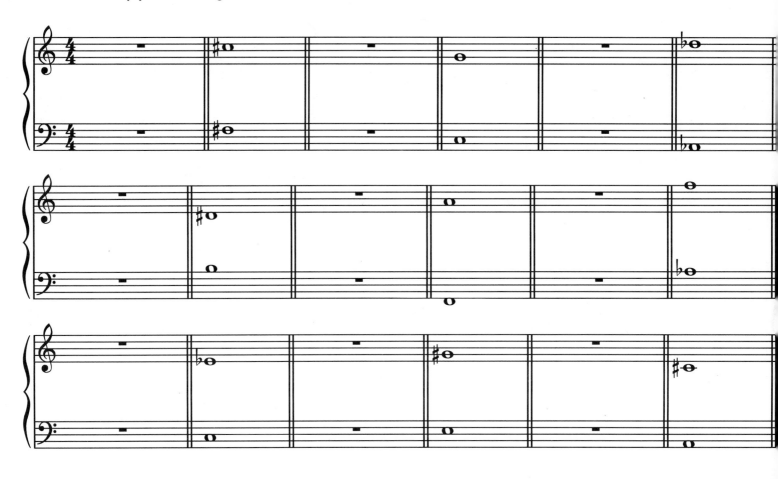

3. Play these folksongs.

Skip to My Lou

American
Arranged by M. Hilley

Bells of London

British
Arranged by M. Hilley

IMPROVISING

1. Discuss the improvisation sections before you play the following ensemble on page 108.

The rest of this page has been left blank to avoid difficult page turns.

Take a Break

L.F.O.

PERFORMANCE

1. Pay close attention to alternating staccato and legato in *Dance* on page 110.

Dance

L.F.O.

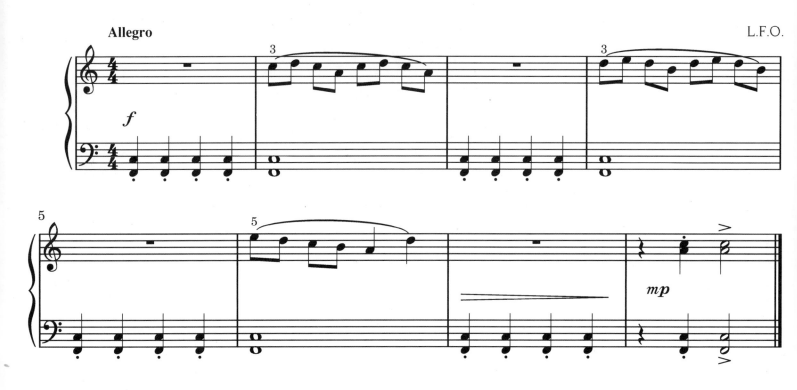

2. Notice clef signs before playing.

Allegro

CORNELIUS GURLITT, Op. 117, No. 5
(1820–1901)

3. Perform as your teacher adds an accompaniment.

Waltz
from *The Merry Widow*

FRANZ LEHÁR
(1870–1948)
Arranged by L.F.O.

4. There are "rolled" intervals in measures 5 and 6 of Part 2. Your teacher will demonstrate
   this technique.

Alouette

French
Arranged by L.F.O.

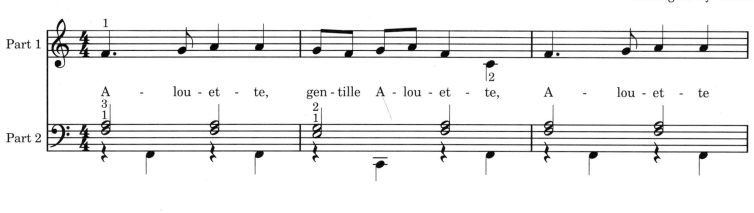

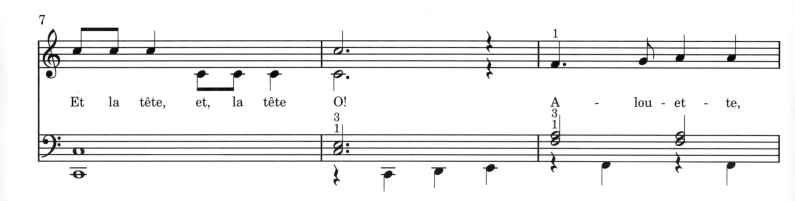

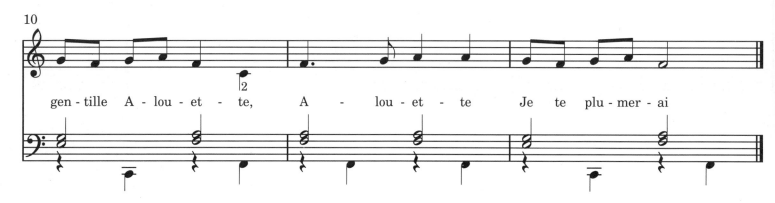

5. Pay careful attention to the pedal indication. On what beat of the measure does it begin?

Song in the Alps

L.F.O.

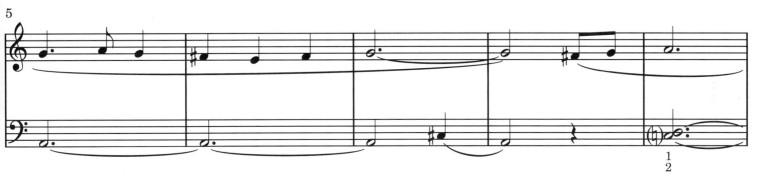

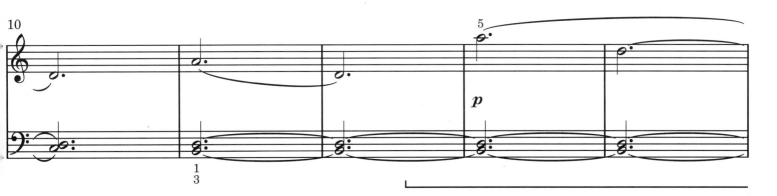

6. Play three times and move to the next part with each playing.

Our Song

WRITING

1. Four different rhythm examples are played on the Cassette. Each example will be played
   three times. Write each one in the space below. Begin with light rhythm shorthand.

7-1

a.

b.

c.

d.

2. Each row represents a major pentascale. Fill in the blanks. Pentascales use consecutive
   letter names.

A   B   ___   ___   E

C   ___   ___   ___   G

D   ___   ___   G   ___

G   ___   ___   ___   ___

F   ___   A♭   ___   ___

8.

Recap

1. Notice clef changes.

Melancholy

L.F.O.

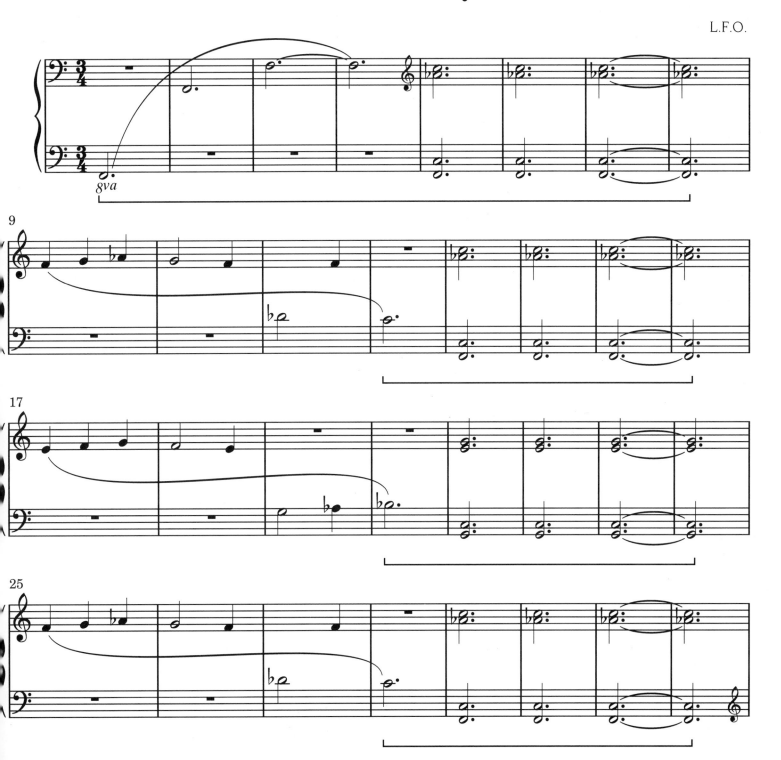

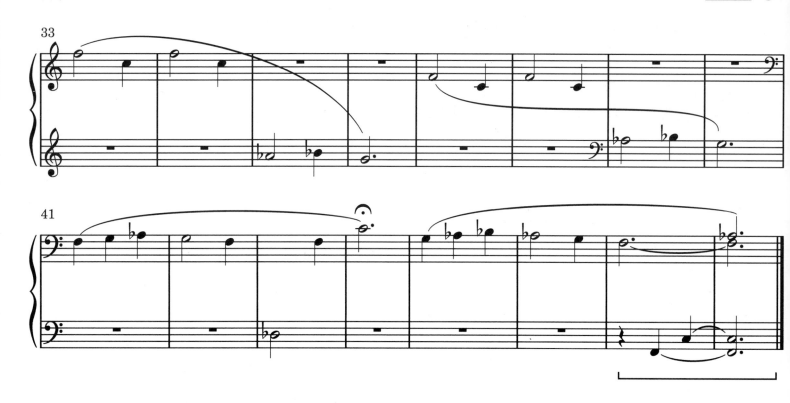

2. Notice the use of ties for each separate phrase.

Kentucky Memory

L.F.O.

3. Perform twice, changing parts for second time around.

Lightly Row

Traditional
Arranged by M. Hilley

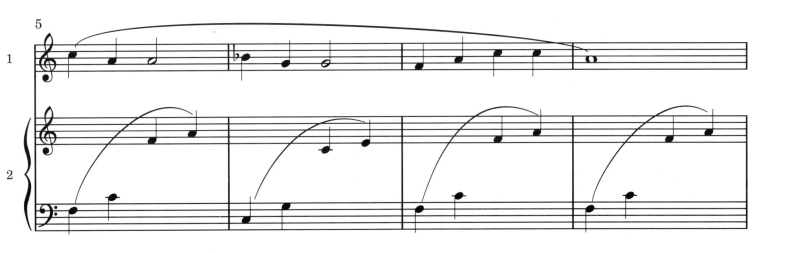

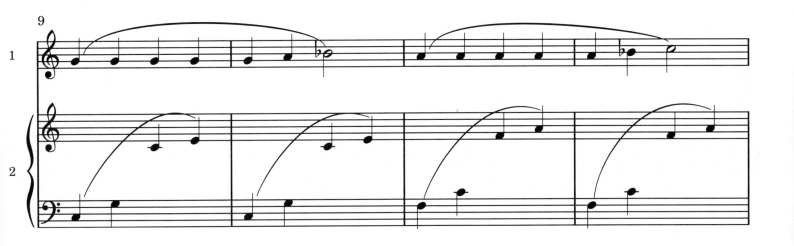

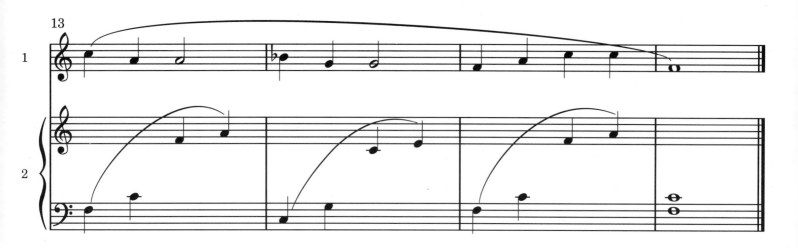

4. Supply fingerings.

Sonatina Breve

L.F.O.

5. Strive for a legato tone.

Aura Lee

American
Arranged by L.F.O.

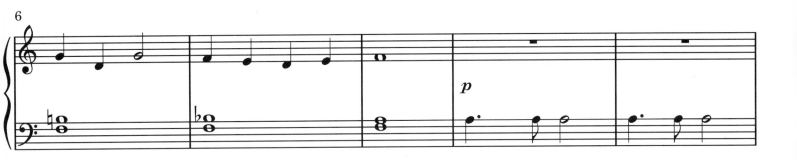

6. Pay careful attention to articulation.

Li'l Liza Jane

Arranged by M. Hilley

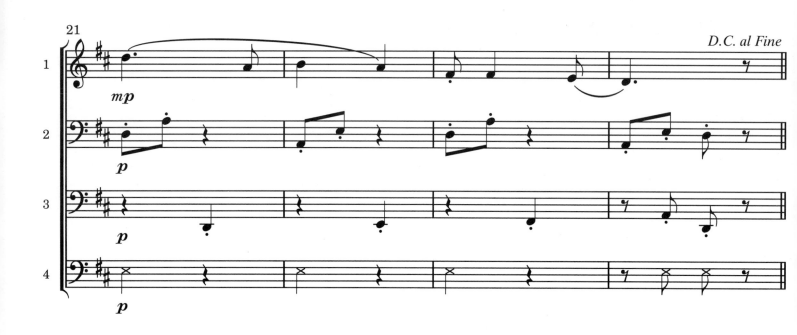

D.C. al Fine

TERMINOLOGY REVIEW

Discuss the following musical terms:

- Treble clef/bass clef
- Grand staff
- Interval
- Broken and blocked intervals
- *Andante/allegro/lento/vivace*
- Phrase/accent/slur
- Sharp/flat/natural
- Half step/whole step
- Scale/pentascale/major pentascale
- *mf/mp*
- Upbeat
- Repeat sign
- Enharmonic
- Staccato/legato

WRITING REVIEW

1. On the keyboard segment, write the letter names of the following major pentascales.

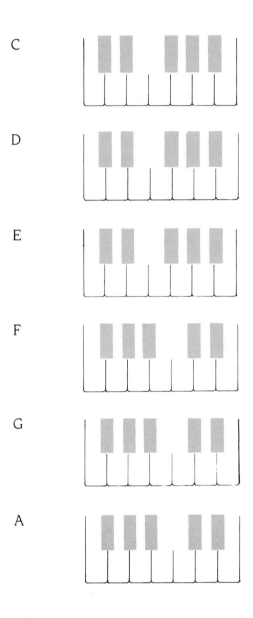

126

9.

Extensions/Triads/Ledger Lines

LISTENING

ff	Fortissimo	Very loud
pp	Pianissimo	Very soft

Moderato	Moderate tempo
Allegretto	A little less *allegro*

1. Listen carefully as your teacher randomly plays portions of the following musical examples. Identify which are played.

Echoing

LOUIS KÖHLER
(1820–1886)

Rigaudon

ALEXANDER GOEDICKE
(1877–1957)

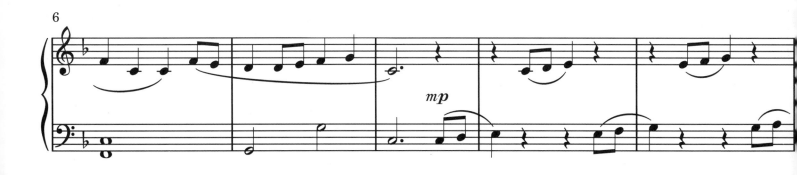

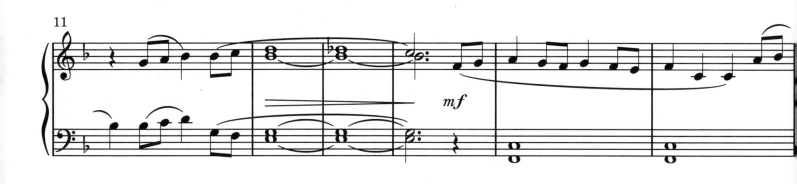

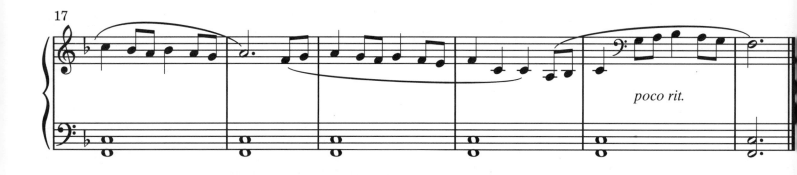

Quiet Conversation

L.F.O.

2. You will hear several examples based on pentascales. Close your book and listen as your teacher gives instructions for the playbacks.

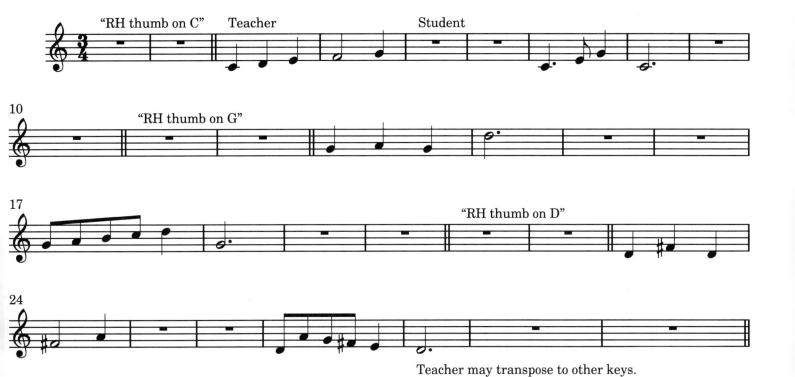

Teacher may transpose to other keys.

RHYTHM

 Tap the following two-handed rhythm exercises as the Cassette provides a background.

9-1

1.

2.

3.

4.

5.

TECHNIQUE

1. Play the following pentascale pieces.

d. **Sturdily**

2. On a flat surface, play LH 5 4 3 2 1. Play again; this time "roll" on the corner of your
thumb so that the other fingers move as a unit slightly to the right:

5   4   3   2   ①
                  roll

When you roll, your fourth finger will be in line with your thumb:

Begin: 5 4 3 2 ①
                      (5 4 3)
Roll back: 5 4 3 2 ①

Now play a major pentascale on the keyboard. When you cross, your second finger will play a
whole step above the pattern.

Smoothly

A major

G major

D major

LH 5   continue

C major

LH 5   continue

Practice a RH crossing by rolling on your thumb. Play a major pentascale upward and downward. When you return to the thumb, roll as you did with the LH but play a half step below with finger 2.

Play also in D, E, F, G, and A major.

3. Study the following locations. Then play each example with the single hand indicated.

a.

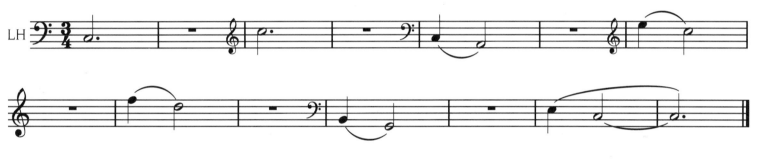

b.

c.

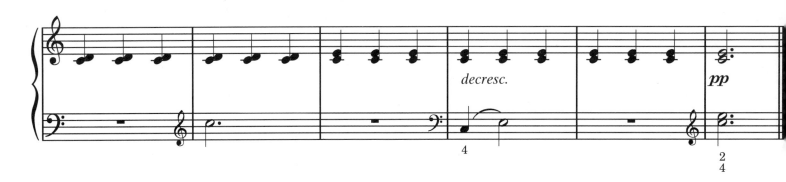

THEORY

> **Triad** The first, third, and fifth tones of a pentascale. The first tone is called "root."

1. Study the two examples shown below. Play the pentascale followed by the root, third, and fifth tones of the pentascale (broken triad). Then play the blocked triad.

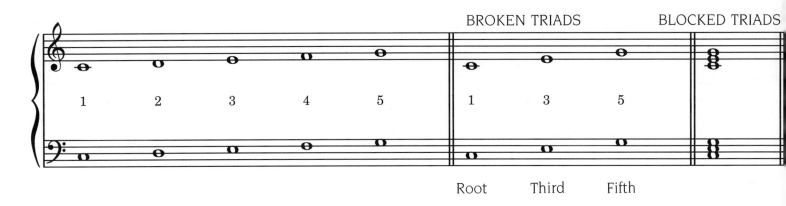

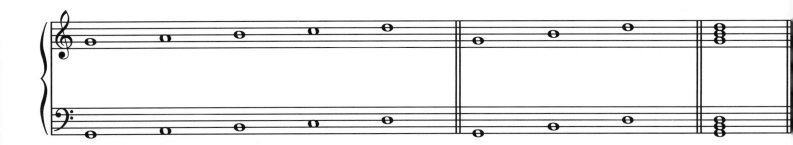

Complete the following examples in the same manner.

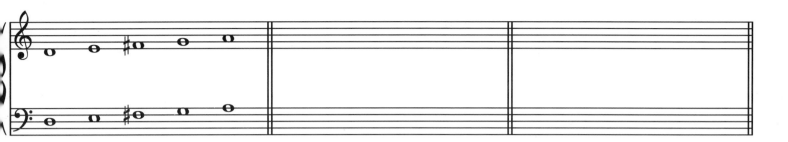

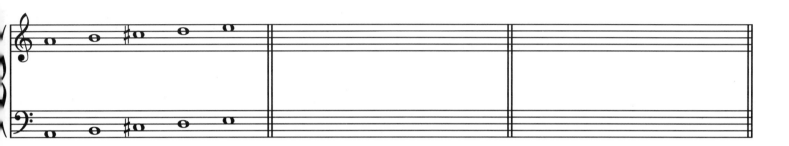

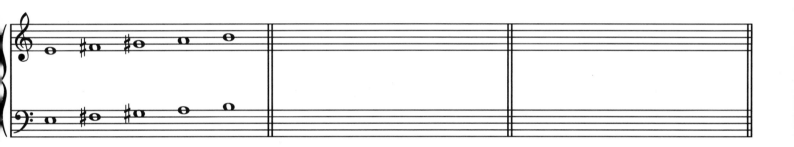

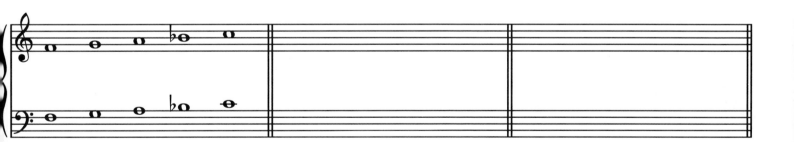

Now play the pentascale/triad exercise in all six keys nonstop. Your teacher will determine the order.

2. Play RH triads and LH root tones for all six keys. C is given as an example. Your teacher will determine the order.

READING

> **Ledger Lines**   Used to indicate pitches above or below the five lines of the staff

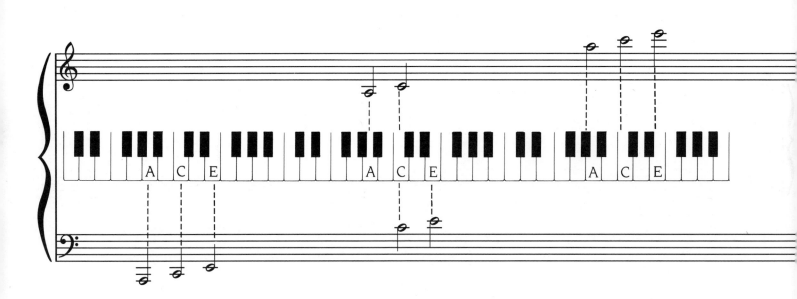

1. During the open measures, locate the next position. Play.

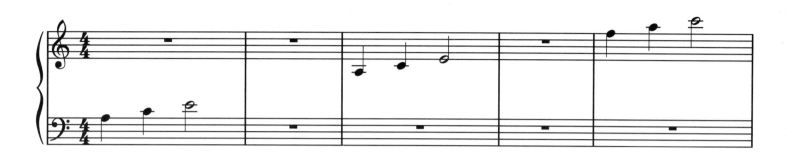

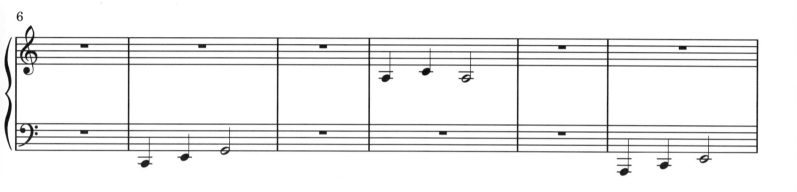

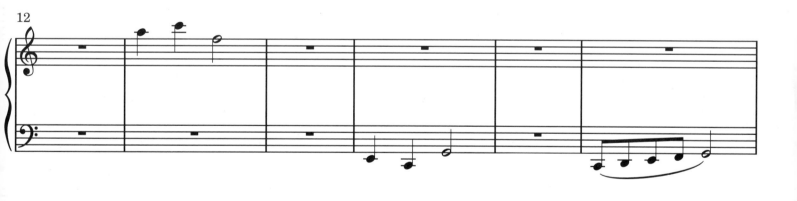

2. Play as written.

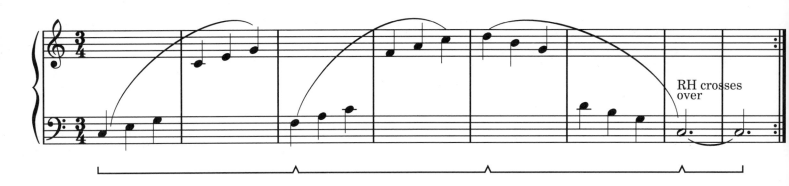

3. For each of the following, circle another group of notes identical in sound to the circled group; then play each example in its entirety after determining fingering.

a.

b.

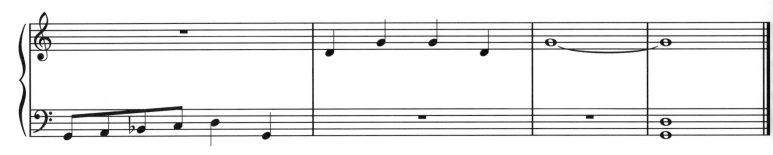

c.

d.

e.

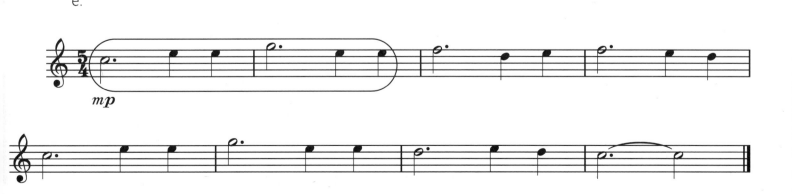

IMPROVISING

1. Improvise on triad tones with RH.

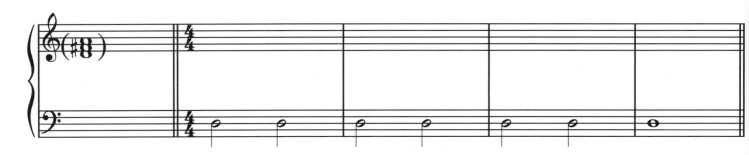

2. Your teacher will demonstrate different two-measure rhythms. Echo the rhythm by playing various tones of a pentascale. The pentascale will be determined by your teacher. Your final bar of improvisation should come to rest on the lowest tone of the pentascale. Close your book!

Teacher (clap or tap)   Student (play)

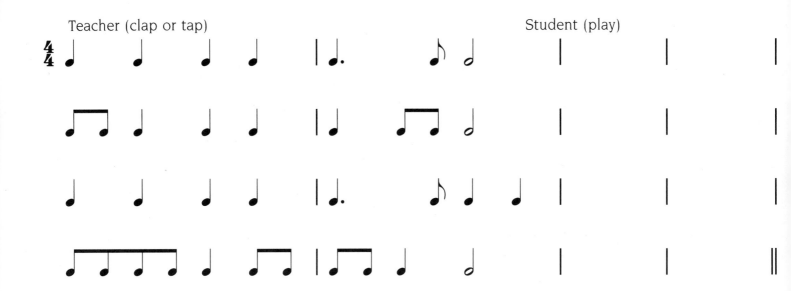

PERFORMANCE

Bell Towers of France

French
Arranged by L.F.O.

Or - lé - ans,   Beau - gen - cy,   No - tre   Dam - e

de   Cler - y,   Ven - dôm - e,   Ven - dôm - e.

For Nine Players (or more)

1. Three players perform melody in unison: one where written, one higher, one lower.

2. Expand to a three-part round, three players for each part: one where written, one higher, one lower. Continue until part 3 plays the melody three times through.

3. Low group divides into three accompaniment figures.

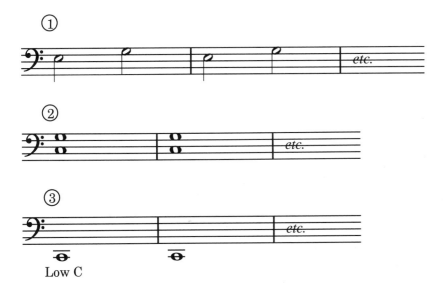

Low C

High group divides into three figures.

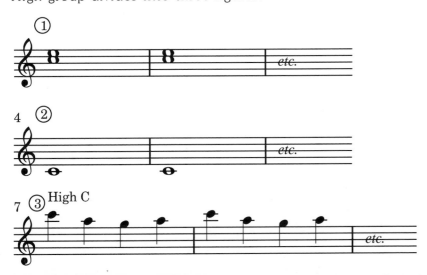

High C

Hickory Breeze

L.F.O.

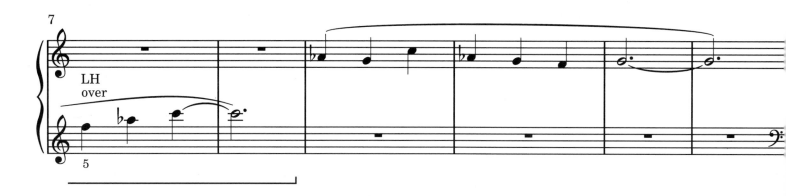

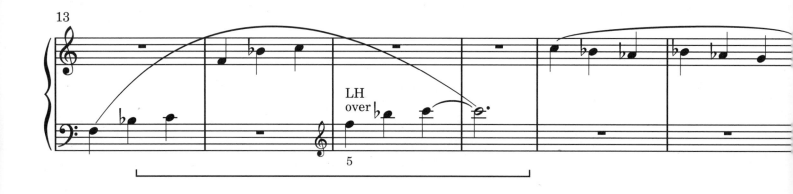

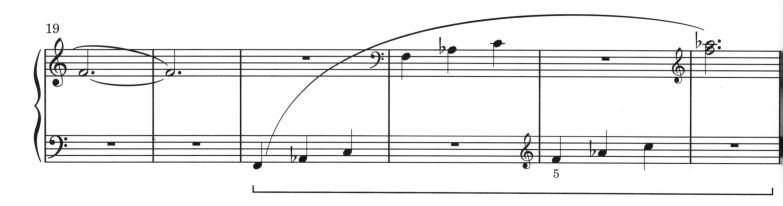

Echoing
(See page 127)

I Know Where I'm Going

Irish
Arranged by M. Hilley

Short Run

L.F.O.

Sunshine Serenade

L.F.O.

WRITING

1. Write triads on each staff using the first, third, and fifth tones of the indicated major pentascale.

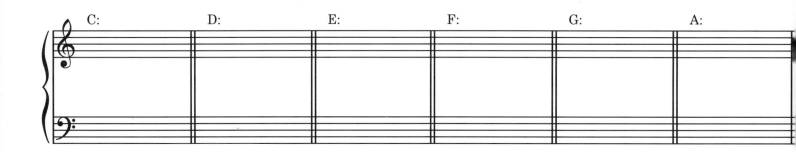

2. Compose a melody to go with the following ostinato. Play hands together.

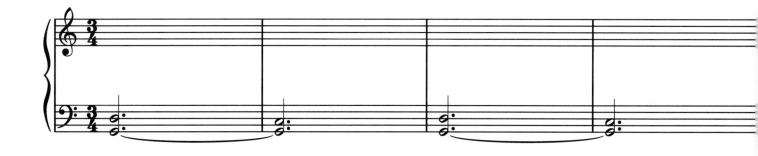

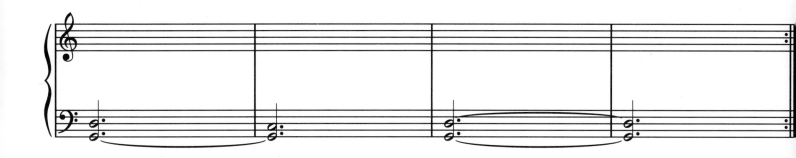

10.

Syncopation/Sixths, Sevenths, Eighths/Major Scales/Key Signatures

LISTENING

1. Locate the indicated keyboard position. Your teacher will play two-measure phrases, each beginning on D; there will be three beats to each measure. After your teacher has played the first two measures, sing back the phrase (use "la" or "loo," etc.). Your teacher will play the first two measures once again; now play these two measures on the keyboard. The same procedure will follow throughout the piece. Close your book!

Ear Investment No. 1

WOODY BUDNICK

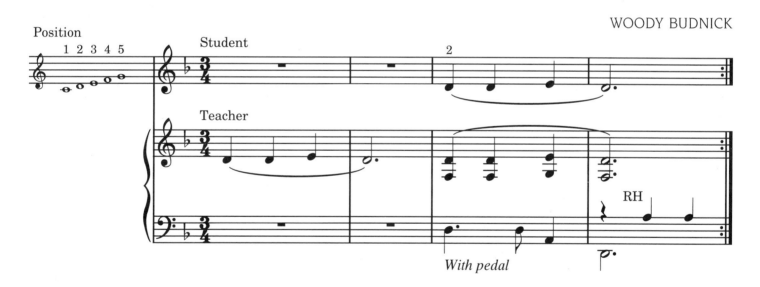

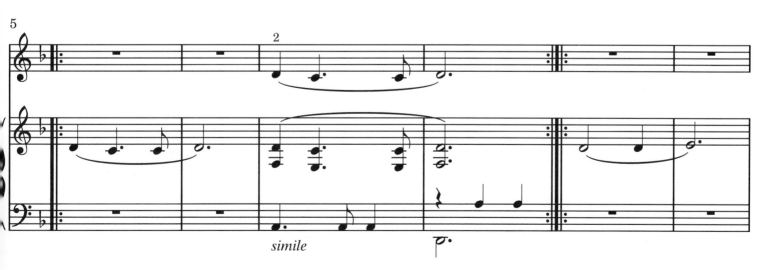

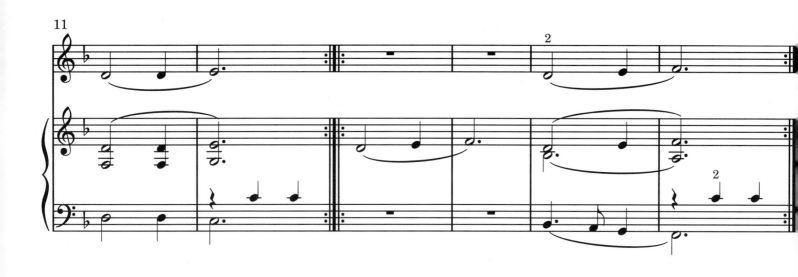

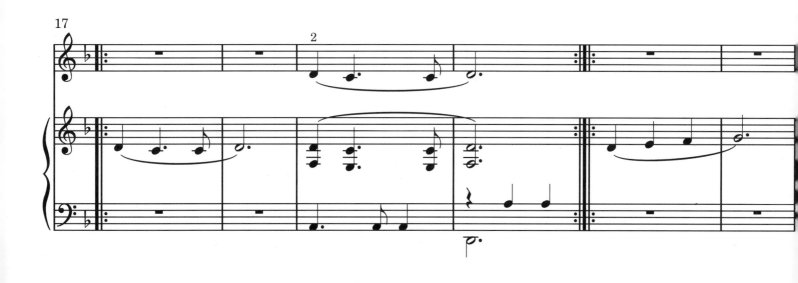

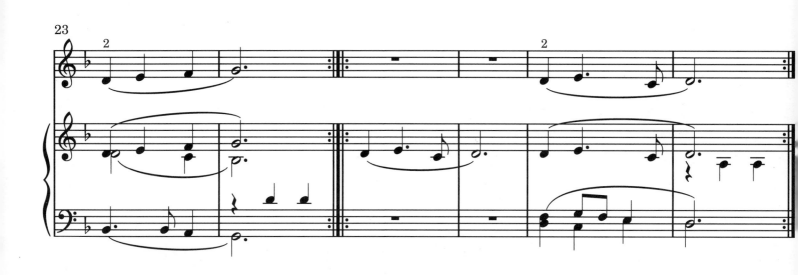

2. Listen as your teacher plays melodic half steps and whole steps. Identify each example as a half step or whole step. If it sounds like the beginning of a major pentascale, it is a whole step; if it sounds smaller, it is a half step. Close your book!

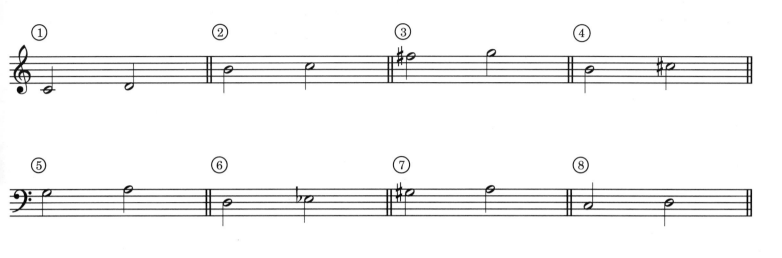

RHYTHM

> **Syncopation** An emphasis on off-beats or weak beats

1. Tap and count aloud the following syncopated rhythm examples.

> ⌢ **Fermata**   Hold longer than the note value

2. Tap these rhythms that use *fermata*.

TECHNIQUE

1. You can extend the pentascale beyond the five-note range in two ways:

    By moving your thumb away from your hand:

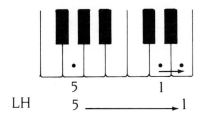

By moving your hand away from your thumb:

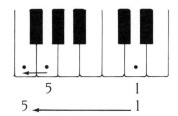

5 1
5 1

With each hand, practice extending the following pentascale positions two ways.

THEORY

1. From C to A is an interval of a sixth. Why?

C D E F G A

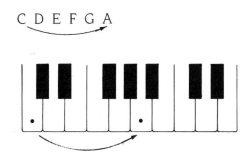   

From C to B is an interval of a seventh. Why?

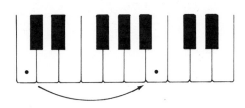 

From C to C is an interval of an eighth (octave). Why?

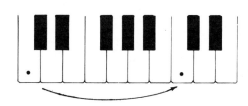 

Play and say the following interval drills.

- Begin with the lowest A on your keyboard and say letter names as you play up in sixths.

- Begin with the lowest B and say letter names as you play up in sevenths.

- Begin with the lowest C and say letter names as you play up in octaves.

- Begin with the highest C and say letter names as you play down in sixths.

- Begin with the highest B and say letter names as you play down in sevenths.

2. A *major key* uses the tones of the major pentascale plus two additional tones.

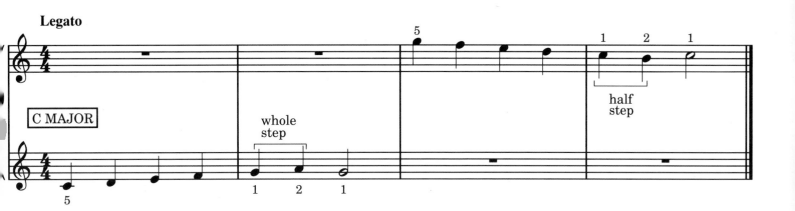

> **Key**   A group of related tones named for their home tone (keynote, or tonic)
>
> **Leading Tone**   The tone that just precedes the tonic

A major scale can be built beginning on any white or black key. For now we will focus on six scales beginning on white keys. Above, you played all tones in the key of C major. No black keys were used. The complete C-major scale looks like this:

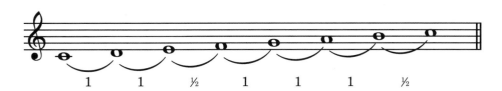

This is the pattern of the whole steps and half steps for all major scales.

Play the two-handed exercises on each of the following keys; then write the scale. Why will the black keys always be *sharps*?

G D A E

F major uses a flat.

The sharps or flats used in each scale may be shown on the staff in a traditional order.

Key Signature   A list of the sharps or flats used in a key

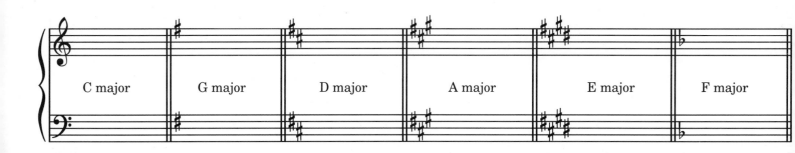

| C major | G major | D major | A major | E major | F major |

3. Play *Jingle Bells* with LH major triads.

Jingle Bells

JAMES PIERPONT
(1822–1893)

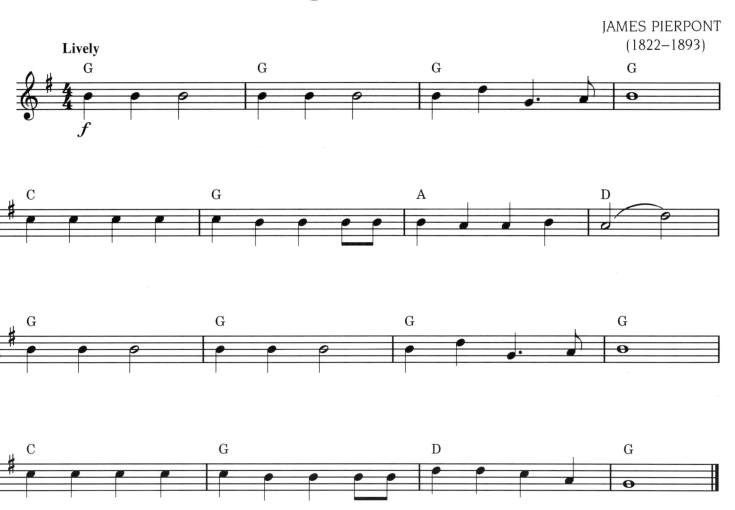

READING

1. The key signature influences notes of the same name, no matter where they appear. Before playing, notice all notes that will be sharped or flatted.

a.

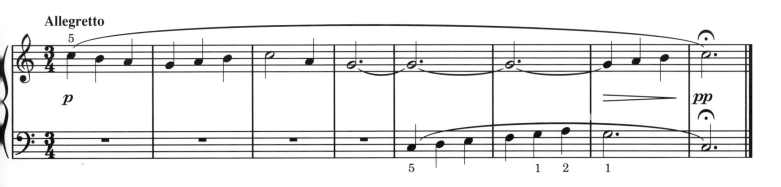

b.

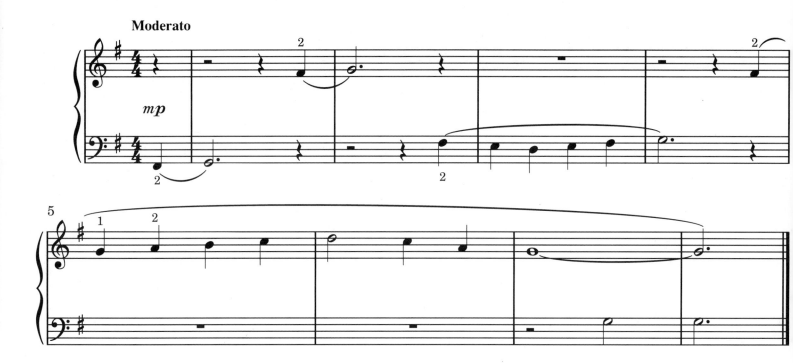

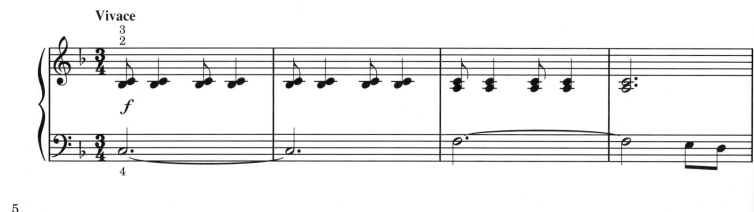

c.

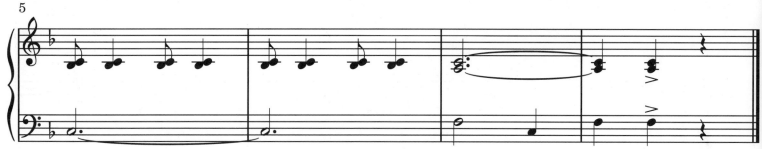

d.

e.

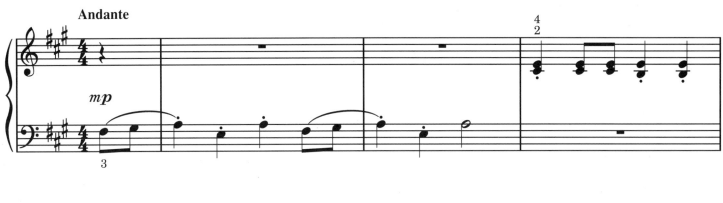

f.

2. Scan the range of each group; plan fingering; play. Use right hand in treble staff, left hand in bass staff.

3. Plan for hand shifts in left hand.

The Riddle Song

British
Arranged by M. Hilley

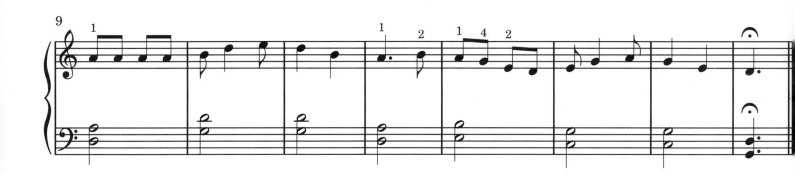

4. Discover extensions before playing.

This Old Man

Traditional
Arranged by M. Hilley

IMPROVISING

1. The "blues pentascale" alters a major pentascale:

$1 - (\text{omit } 2) - \flat 3 - 4 - \flat 5 - \natural 5$

Play the blues pentascales on C, F, and G.

Improvise a melody using the C blues pentascale as your teacher provides a background (shown on next page).

Teacher Background

PERFORMANCE

Study: Changing Hand Position

from *The First Term at the Piano*

BÉLA BARTÓK
(1881–1945)

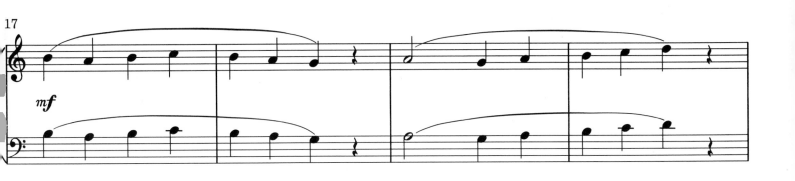

Twilight

L.F.O.

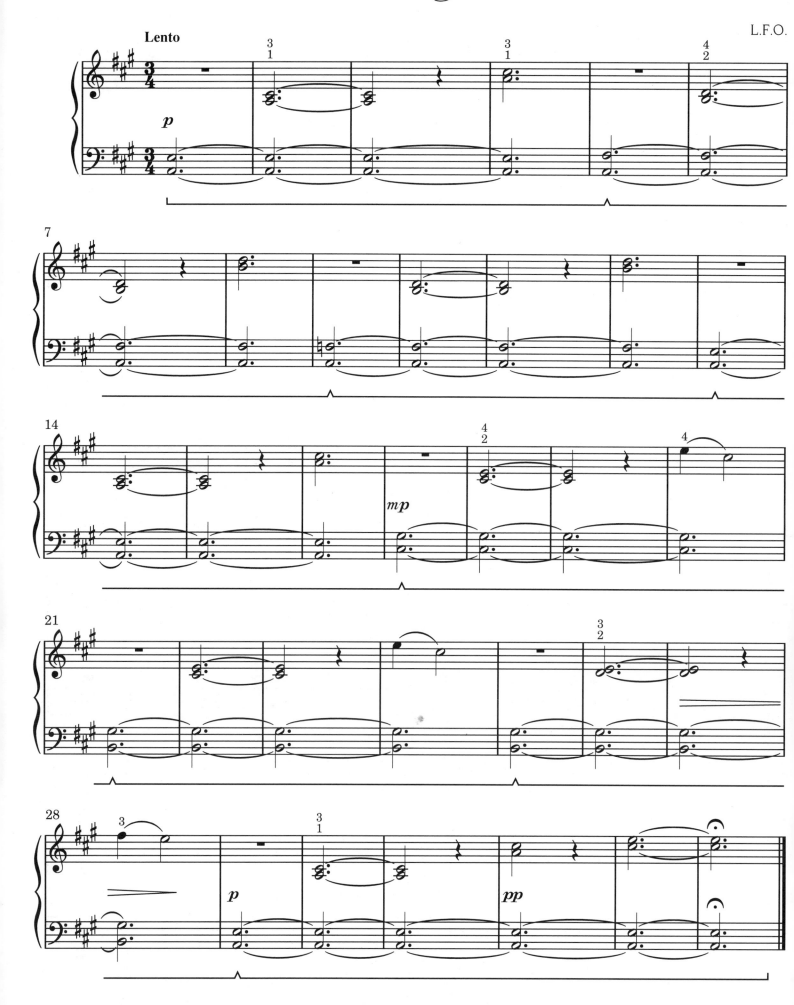

Scratchy Band

The Coventry Carol

Arranged by Katherine Beard

Gently, like a lullaby

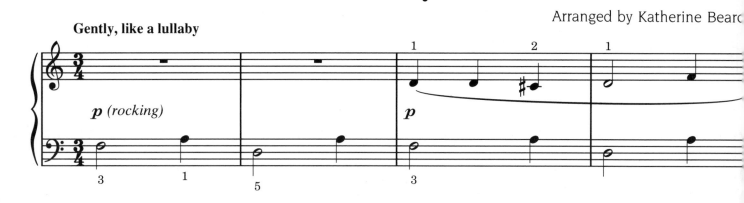

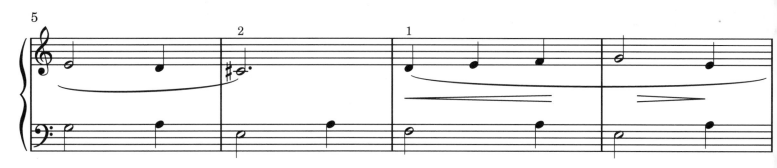

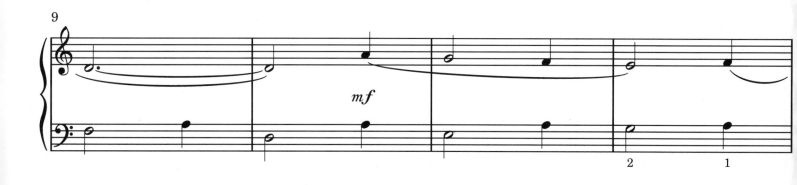

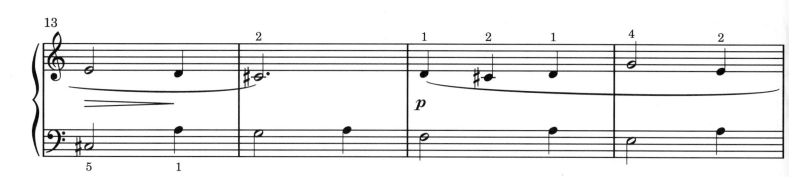

WRITING

1. Circle any notes that would be sharps or flats. (Do not play.)

2. Copy each of the given clefs and key signatures. Name the major key.

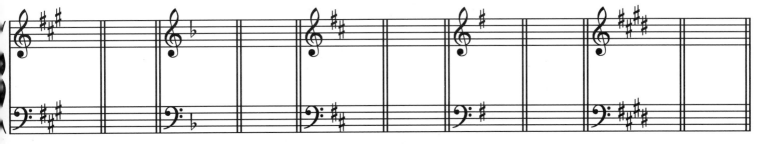

170

11.

Scale Fingering/Primary Chords/Harmonizing/ Transposing

LISTENING

Pesante	Heavily
Leggiero	Lightly
Cantabile	Singing
Marcato	With marked emphasis
Andantino	A little faster than andante
Scherzando	Playfully

11-1
1. Listen carefully to the six musical examples on the Cassette. Determine which example is played *pesante*, which is played *leggiero*, which is played *cantabile*, which is played *marcato*, which is played *andantino*, and which is played *scherzando*.

RHYTHM

Select sounds. Consider clapping, tapping, knocking wood, striking metal, etc.

Fly Away

L.F.O.

TECHNIQUE

1. Practice this traditional RH fingering for the C-major scale, two octaves.

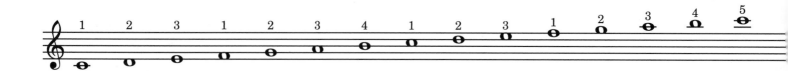

Now look carefully at this traditional LH fingering for the C-major scale.

The fingering shown above is used for the following major scales: C D E G A.

Play each of the scales, hands separately, two octaves up and back down.

2. Play the following melodic and harmonic interval exercises.

a.

b.

c.

d.

e.

f.

g.

h.

i.

j.

3. During each rest, prepare the next blocked interval with hand away from the keyboard.

a.

b.

4. Play these technique studies; keep your hand relaxed.

a.

b.

c.

d.

e.

f.

THEORY

> **Tonic**   Home tone or keynote
>
> **Dominant**   Fifth tone of a scale
>
> **Subdominant**   Fourth tone of scale

1. In a major pentascale, the bottom tone is called tonic (I) and the top tone is called dominant (V). The subdominant (IV) is the fourth tone.

Generally, when a melody is made mostly of tones 1, 3, and 5, you would accompany with tonic (I); when the melody is mostly 2 and 4, you would accompany with dominant (V); when the melody centers on 4 alone, you have the option of dominant (V) or subdominant (IV). Your ear will always be the final test of appropriate accompaniment.

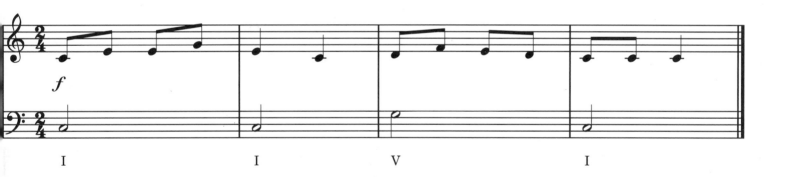

I   I   V   I

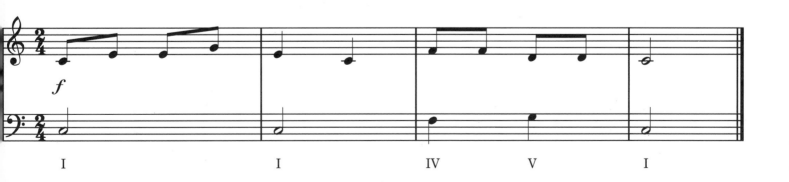

I   I   IV   V   I

To accompany right-hand melodies, you may choose to use the left-hand pentascale position as illustrated. We also encourage the frequent use of dominant and subdominant *below* tonic. This is easy when you place your left-hand thumb on a white-key tonic.

2. Accompany the following melodies with tonic, dominant, and subdominant tones. Try both "dominant/subdominant above" and "dominant/subdominant below" left-hand positions.

3. Tonic (I), dominant (V), and subdominant (IV) triads are built on the first, fifth, and fourth tones of the scale. Play the following exercises using I, V, and IV triads. Spell the next triad aloud during each measure of rest.

a.

I   ⟶   V   ⟶   I   ⟶   V   ⟶   I

b.

I   ⟶   IV   ⟶   I   ⟶   IV   ⟶   I

c.

I   ⟶   IV   ⟶   I   ⟶   V   ⟶   I

d.

I   ⟶   IV   ⟶   V   ⟶   V   ⟶   I

e.

I   ⟶   IV   ⟶   V   ⟶   V   ⟶   I

Play the harmonic patterns again using these major keys: D E F G A.

Transposition Writing and/or performing music in a key other than the original key. When you transpose, you think the new key and intervals.

F major

mp

G major

mp

4. Play the following C-major exercise; then play in the keys of G major and D major.

f

5. Transpose the Bartók *Legato Study* to the keys of F major and A major.

Legato Study
from *The First Term at the Piano*

BÉLA BARTÓK
(1881–1945)

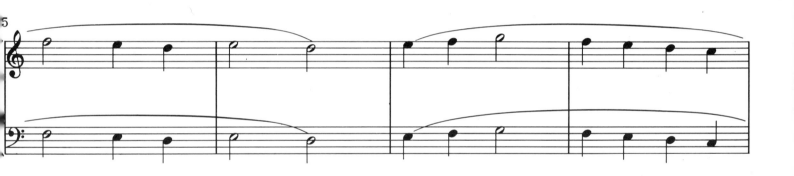

READING

Etude in G

L.F.O

Scherzando

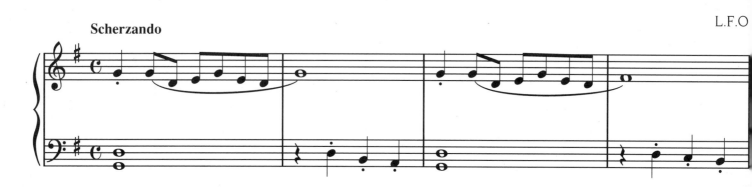

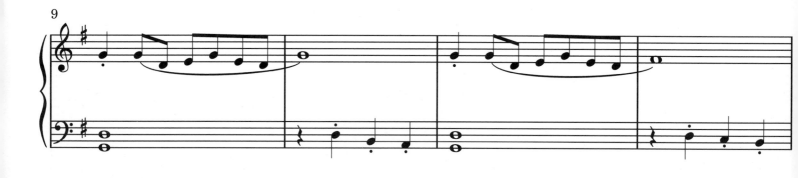

LH over RH

Bounce

L.F.O.

Southern Tune

American
Arranged by L.F.O.

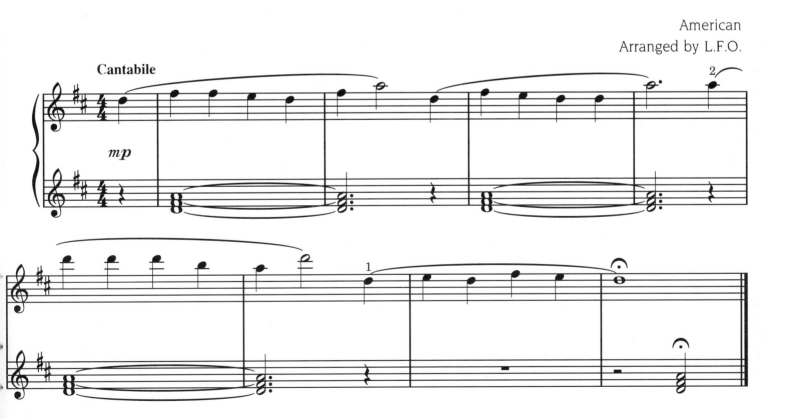

IMPROVISING

1. The RH melody of the following piece uses the C blues pentascale. The LH plays single-tone roots of the harmony shown by Roman numerals. Play as written.

C Blues Pentascale

Play again, this time varying the RH rhythm. For example:

etc.

2. Follow the chord changes below. LH plays single-tone roots; RH improvises using the G blues pentascale (the pentascale never has to change position).

Key of G

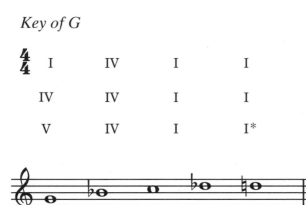

*Notice that the piece and the chart follow the same pattern of single-tone roots.

PERFORMANCE

Largo

ANTON DVOŘÁK
(1841–1904)
Arranged by L.F.O.

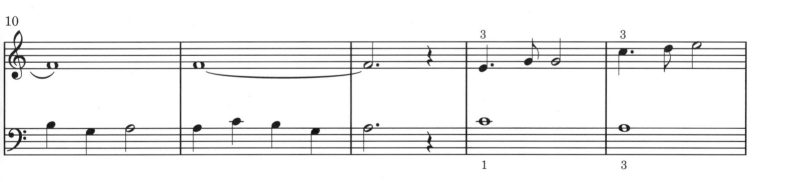

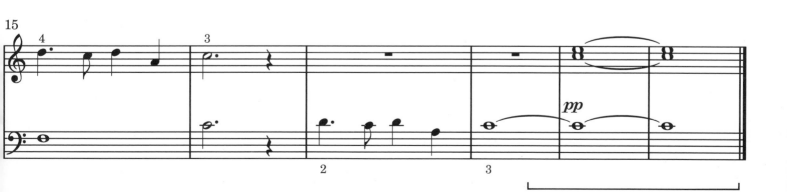

One Four Seven

L.F.C

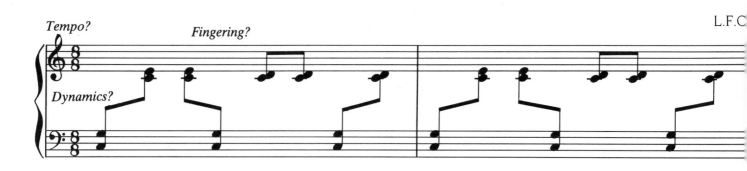

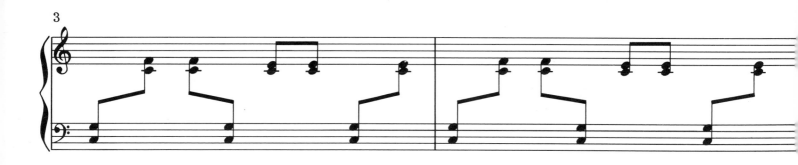

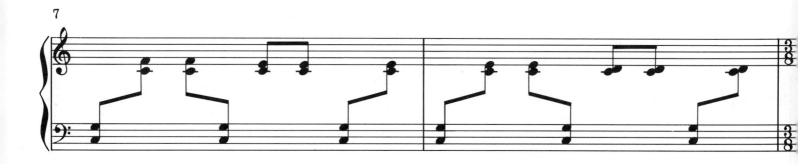

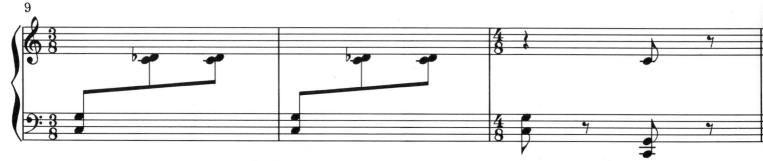

Noon Clouds

L.F.O.

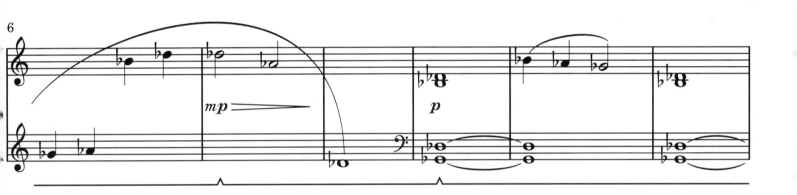

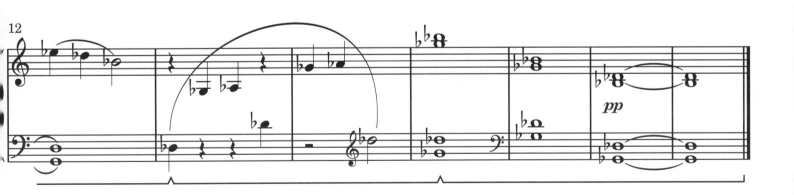

A Little Joke

from 24 *Pieces for Children*

DMITRI KABALEVSKY, Op. 39, No. 6
(1904–1987)

*A short line (–) by a notehead indicates emphasis by sustaining. In this case, it makes the *staccato* a bit less short. The Italian word for this sign is *tenuto*.

Wayfarin' Stranger

Arranged by Ann Collins

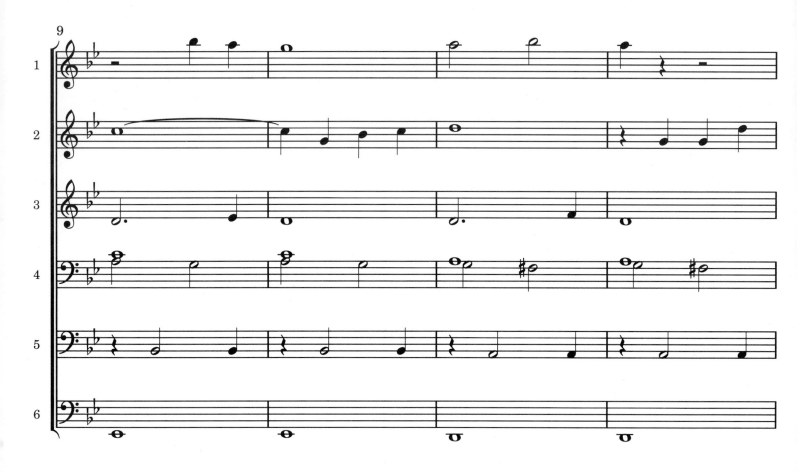

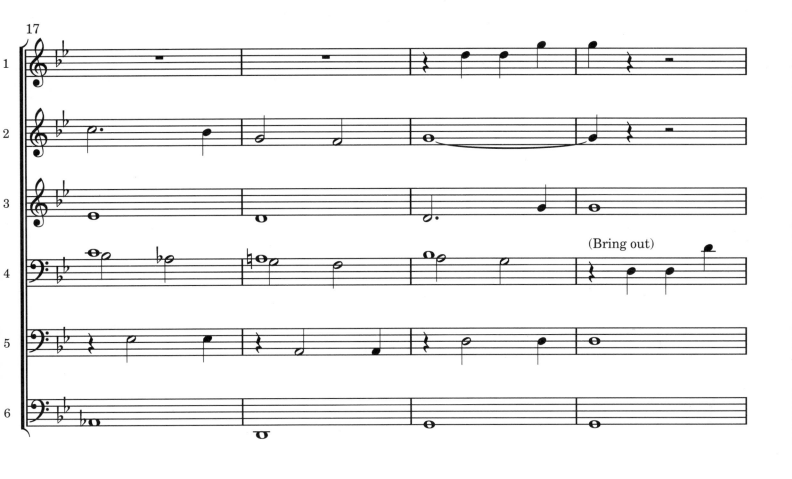

(Bring out)

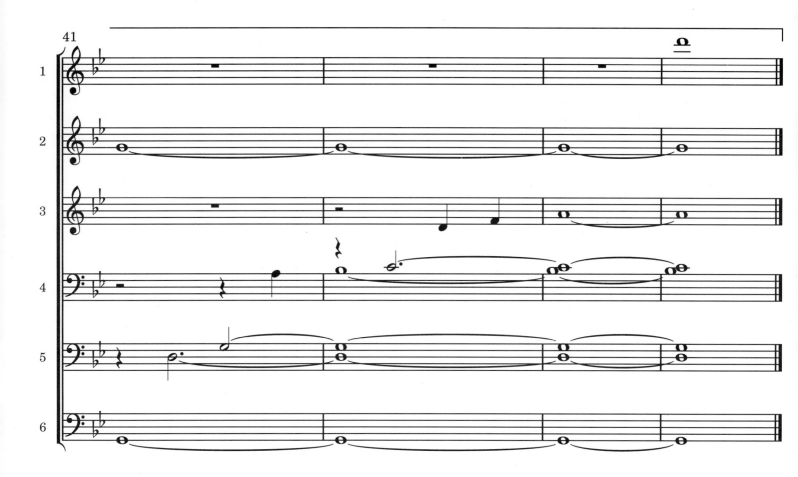

WRITING

1. Write triads for the following major keys. Use necessary sharps or flats with the triads (rather than signatures).

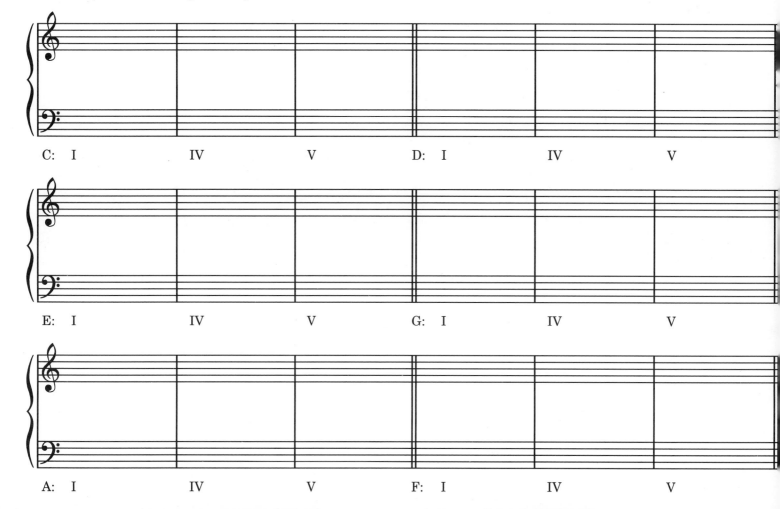

2. Rewrite this melody in D major and C major.

F major

12.

Recap

PERFORMANCE

Razz-Ma-Tazz

L.F.O.

Italian Song

L.F.O.

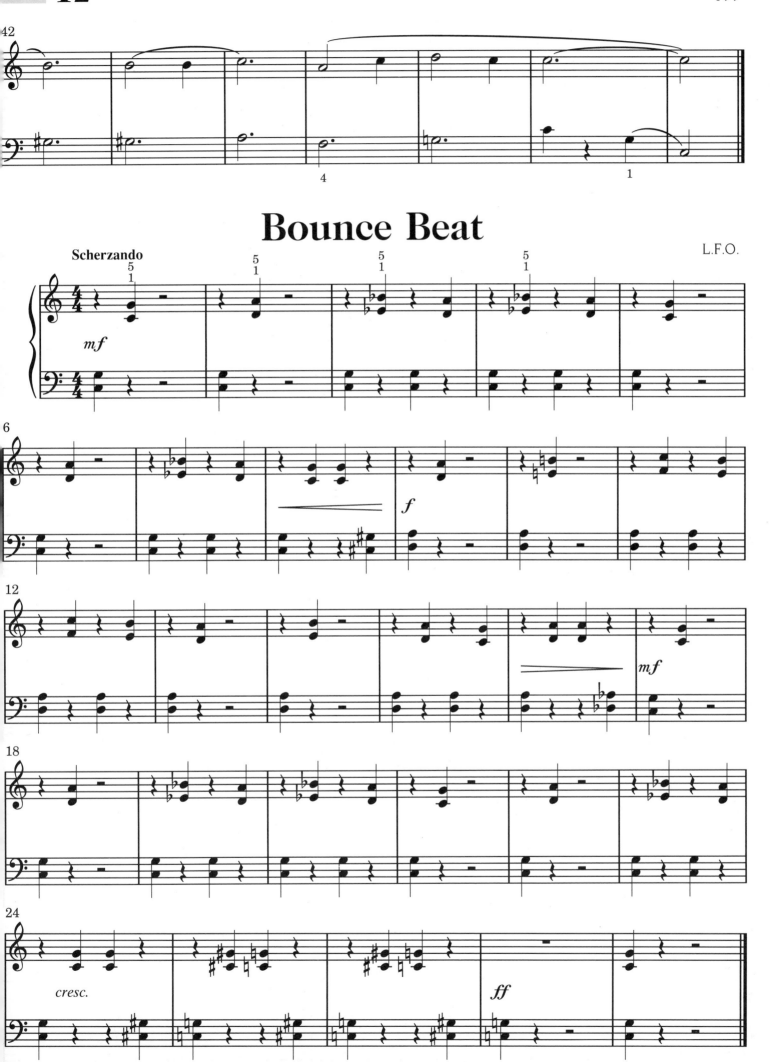

Bounce Beat

L.F.O.

Shepherd Pipes

T. SALUTRINSKAYA

Holiday Song

British
Arranged by L.F.O.

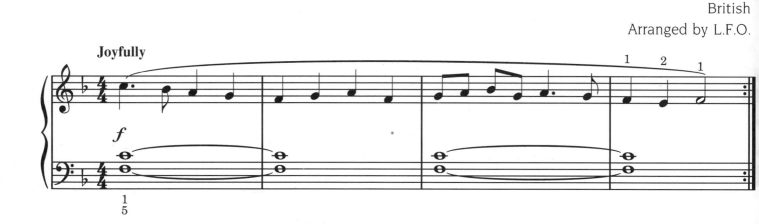

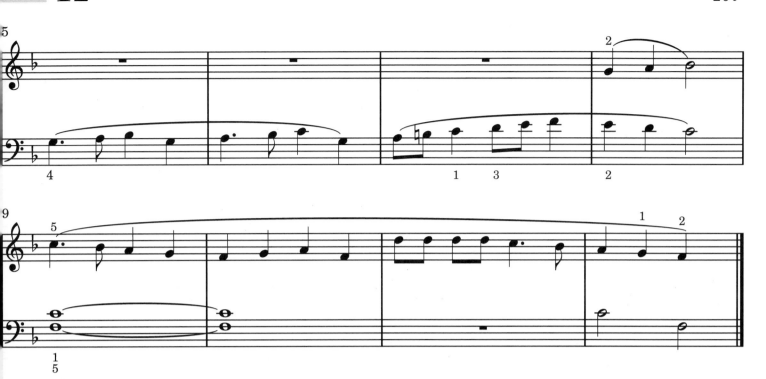

Vesper Song

ROBERT DONAHUE

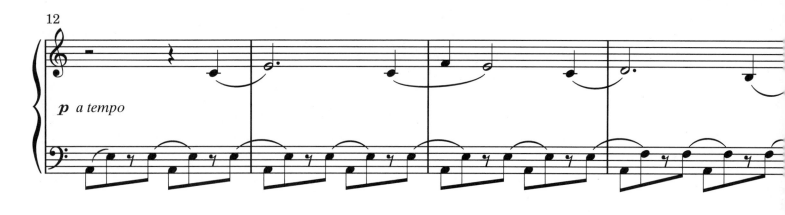

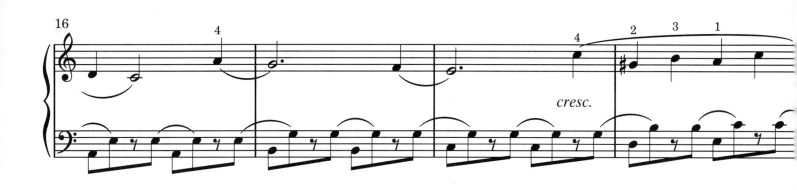

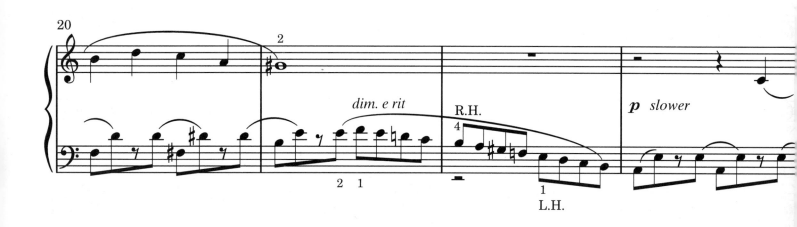

Fanfare
from *Notebook for Wolfgang*

LEOPOLD MOZART
(1719–1787)
Adapted by L.F.O.

Marietta's Song

L.F.O

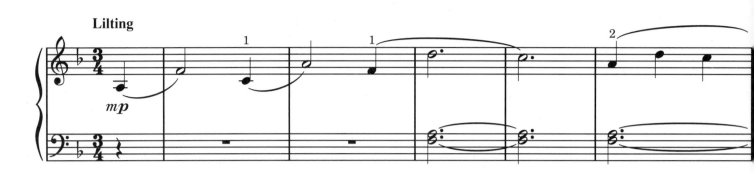

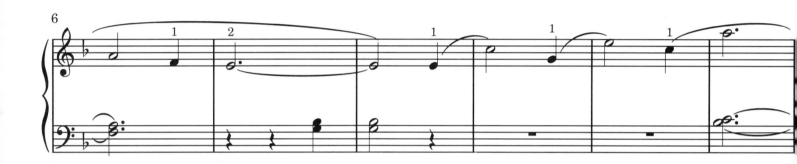

TERMINOLOGY REVIEW

Discuss the following musical terms:

- Triad/root, third, fifth
- Ledger lines
- Syncopation
- Fermata
- Sixths/sevenths/octaves
- Key/key signature
- Leading tone
- Tonic/dominant/subdominant
- *Pesante/leggiero/cantabile/marcato/andantino/scherzando*
- ***ff*** / ***pp***
- Transposition
- *Moderato/allegretto*

WRITING REVIEW

1. Complete the following interval chains by writing the note-name answer.

B, up a 4th   F, down a 2nd
    down a 6th   up a 5th
    up a 3rd   down a 6th
    down a 7th   up a 7th

    _____   _____

D, up a 4th   E, down a 4th
    down a 5th   up a 3rd
    up a 6th   down a 7th
    down a 7th   up a 6th

    _____   _____

2. Write these major scales on the keyboards below.

C

D
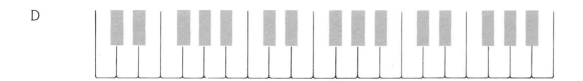

E
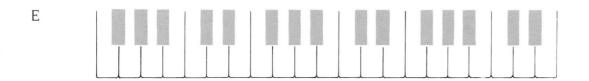

G

A

continued

3. Rewrite the following rhythms with barlines and any necessary ties. The first note is beat one.

a.

$\begin{smallmatrix} 6 \\ 4 \end{smallmatrix}$

b.

$\begin{smallmatrix} 4 \\ 4 \end{smallmatrix}$

c.

$\begin{smallmatrix} 2 \\ 4 \end{smallmatrix}$

d.

$\begin{smallmatrix} 3 \\ 4 \end{smallmatrix}$

208

13.

Chord Inversions/ Guitar Symbols

LISTENING

Ritardando *rit.* Gradual slowing of tempo

Accelerando *accel.* Becoming faster

A tempo To return to the original or previous tempo after such indications as *rit.* or *accel.*

13-1

1. Listen carefully to the three musical examples on the Cassette. As the examples are replayed, determine which examples use *rit.*, *accel.*, and/or *a tempo*.

2. Locate the indicated keyboard position. Your teacher will play two-measure phrases and one final four-measure phrase. After your teacher has played the first phrase, repeat vocally. Your teacher will play the first phrase once again; now play this phrase on the keyboard. The same procedure will follow throughout the piece. Close your book!

Ear Investment No. 2

WOODY BUDNICK

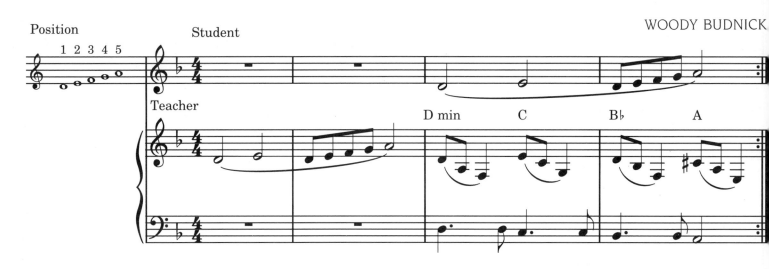

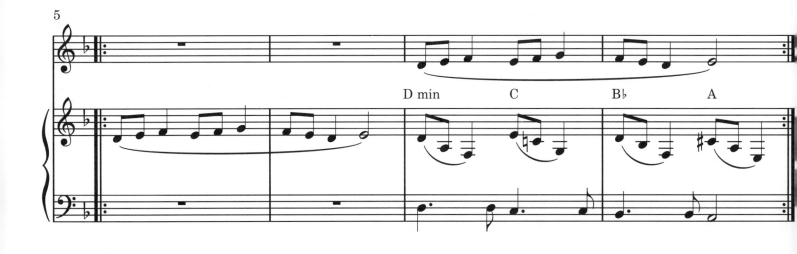

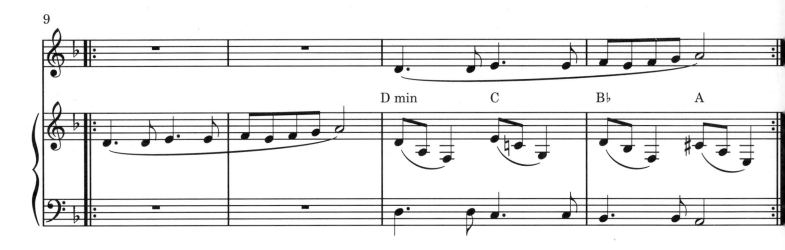

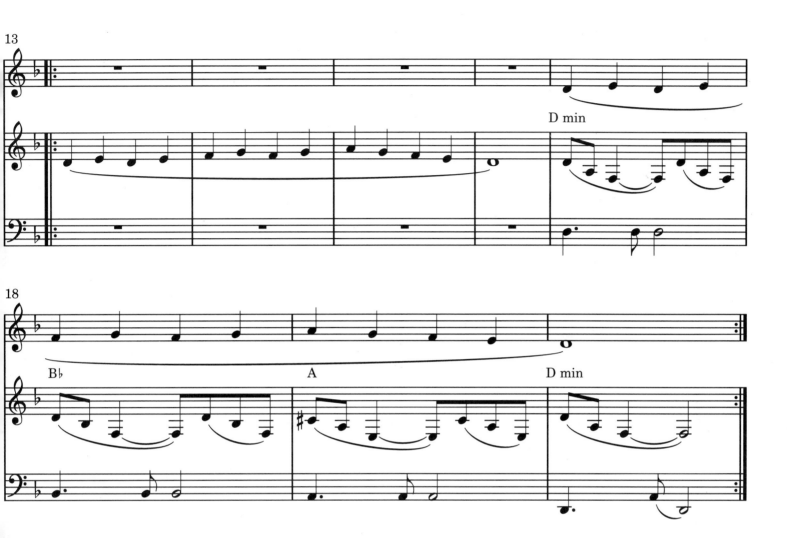

RHYTHM

♪ Eighth Rest   Equivalent to the eighth note in duration

---

1. Tap the following rhythms that use an eighth-note upbeat and an eighth rest.

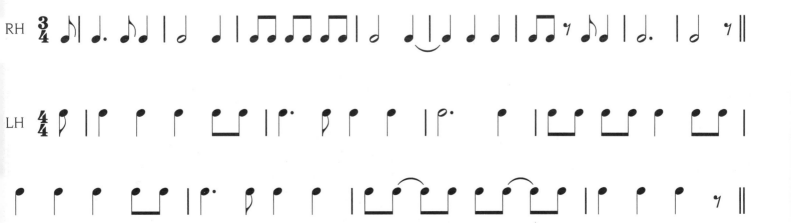

2. Use the following sounds in the $\frac{4}{4}$ rhythm chart:

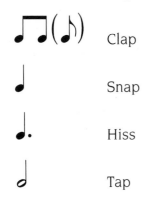

Clap

Snap

Hiss

Tap

Form a rhythm ensemble and perform.

TECHNIQUE

1. Notice chord shapes as you play these exercises.

 2. Review the following scales, hands separately, as the Cassette provides a rhythmic
13-2   background:

C   D   E   G   A

Play the scales once more, this time hands together in *contrary* motion. Use the following
example as a guide.

3. The following phrases use finger crossings. For each, plan a logical fingering that involves a crossing.

a.

b.

c.

d.

e.

4. The following exercises involve wide leaps. To move, look quickly at the keyboard when necessary and, just as quickly, focus again on the printed page.

a. **Moderato**

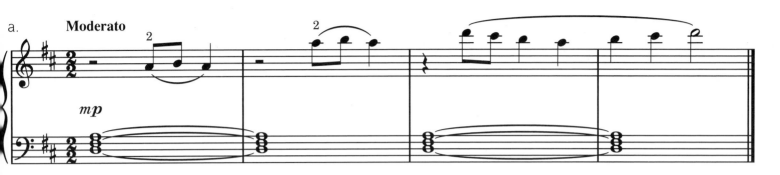

b. **Allegretto**

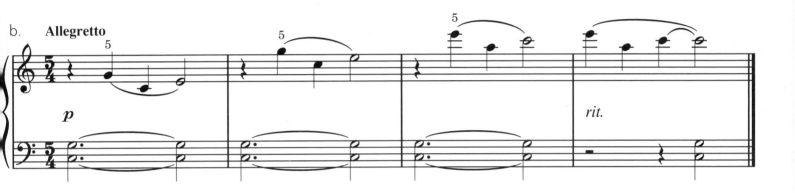

c. **Allegro**

d. **Marcato**

THEORY

1. Chords may be designated in different ways—by Roman numeral as shown in Unit 11 (I, IV, V) or by letter name (usually called guitar symbols). Most popular music will have guitar symbols written above the vocal line. These symbols represent the harmonies that have been used in that particular arrangement.

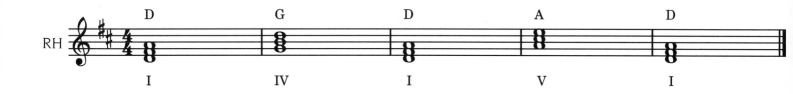

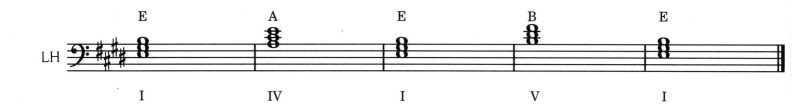

Chord Inversion   Root position rearranged

2. Inverted chords provide economy of motion when moving from one chord to the next. Play through the following "closest possible position" chord exercise.

The shape of inverted chords is designated by figures (Arabic numerals):

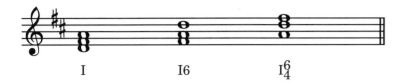

or by letter name:

Chord designations in *Piano for Pleasure* will be primarily guitar symbols.

3. "Closest position" chords share common tones in many instances. Mark the *common tones* in the examples shown below by drawing a line between them.

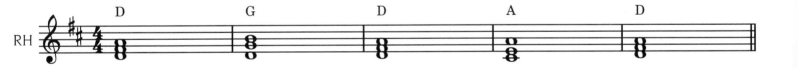

Play the following root position triads followed by their inversions.

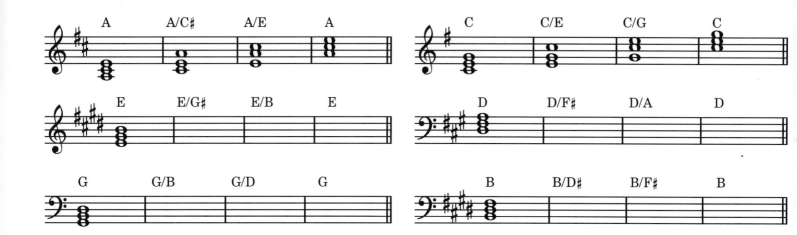

Assign the proper Roman numeral to each root position triad used above.

4. Return to the single tone harmonization in Unit 11 (p. 178) and play again using triads in closest position possible. Think guitar symbols.

READING

1. When reading chords, notice the interval formed by the two "outside" notes; then mentally fill in the other note or notes.

For example:

Notice 6th   Fill in 3rd

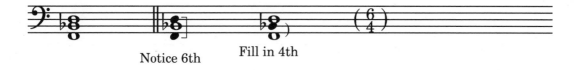

Notice 6th   Fill in 4th

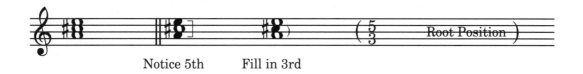

Notice 5th   Fill in 3rd

Use the preceding reading method and play the following exercise.

2. Look for "common tones" in the right-hand accompaniment.

Study in G

LUDVIG SCHYTTE, Op. 108, No. 12
(1848–1909)

3. Half-note pulse will be consistent at the meter changes.

Kum-Bah-Yah

African
Arranged by L.F.O

IMPROVISING

1. Return to *Wayfarin' Stranger* (pp. 189). Divide the class on parts 3, 4, 5, and 6. These parts can accompany melodic improvisation based on the following ideas.

Or you might use some combination of these ideas.

Smoke Signals

OLIVE DUNGAN

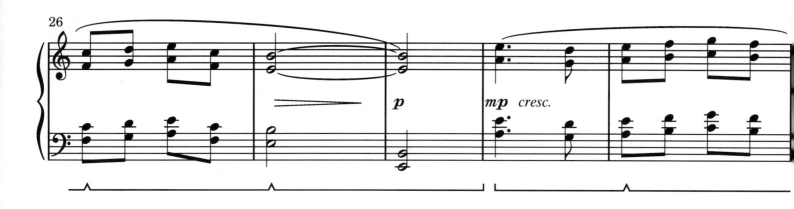

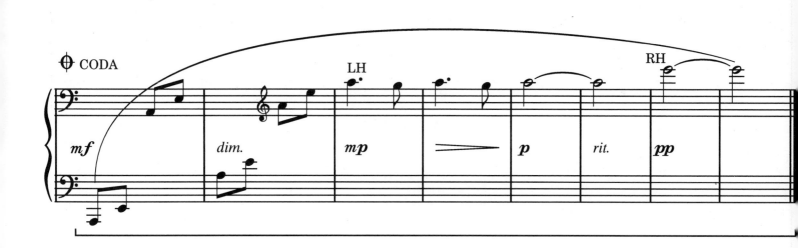

*da capo al ⊕ —back to the beginning, play until ⊕ (a sign indicating *Coda*, and ending)

Beautiful Brown Eyes

Traditional
Arranged by M. Hilley

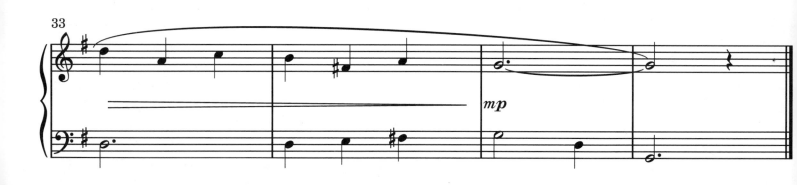

Emotions

JOSEPH M. MARTIN

13

Summer Night

L.F.O.

Rigaudon

(See page 128)

WRITING

1. Furnish the following chords using the principle of closest possible position. Indicate the inversion used. The first exercise gives an example.

a.
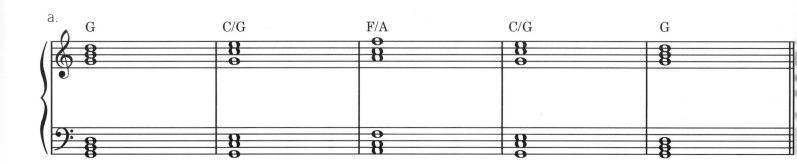

b.
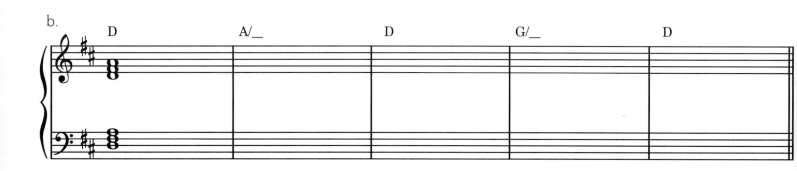

c.
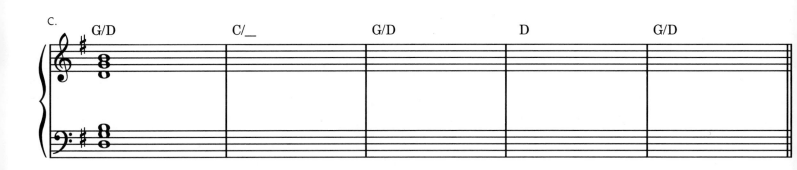

d.
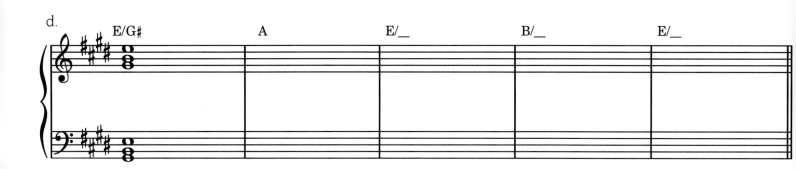

14.

Sixteenth Notes/Interval Quality/Dominant Sevenths

LISTENING

14-1
1. Listen carefully to the several rhythm examples on the Cassette. Tap back after each example.

2. Your teacher will play randomly from the following examples. Be prepared to identify which example is being performed.

RHYTHM

Sixteenth Notes A group of four is equivalent to the duration of a quarter note.

1. Tap the following rhythms using sixteenth notes.

2. Chant and tap the following folk lyric.

Hey, Ho!

English

Next, tap and chant as a group in a rhythm round. Divide into four parts. When part 1 reaches *, part 2 starts at the beginning. When part 1 reaches **, part 3 starts at the beginning. When part 1 reaches ***, part 4 begins.

Continue until each part has completed the lyric twice. Part 4 will finish alone. Each part should tap on a different sounding surface (part 1—piano top; part 2—bench, etc.).

TECHNIQUE

1. Play these examples that use broken triads.

a. **Smoothly**

b. **Smoothly**

c.

poco means ''little''

2. Play this "crossing study" until finger shifts come naturally. Then repeat the exercise in the keys of C, E, G, and A.

3. Study the following fingering for scales, hands together, two octaves. Practice the fingering on a flat surface several times before using it to play the following major scales.

C D E G A

RH: 1 2 3 1 2 3 4 1 2 3 1 2 3 4 5
LH: 5 4 3 2 1 3 2 1 4 3 2 1 3 2 1

THEORY

1. Intervals in music have further qualities than their distance designation. They may be called major, minor, diminished, or augmented. This is determined by the *number* of whole steps and half steps used to build the particular interval.

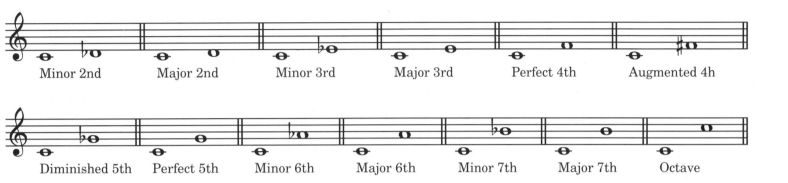

2. Study the triads below and determine the quality of the intervals used.

Example:

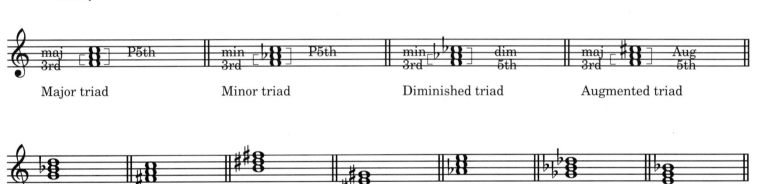

Major triad   Minor triad   Diminished triad   Augmented triad

---

Dominant Seventh   Chord built on fifth degree of the scale. It consists of the dominant triad plus a minor seventh above the root.

---

3. Study the intervals marked in each dominant seventh.

Key of C

4. For *each major key shown*, play a dominant seventh in the right hand.
   Think: tonic; dominant; dominant seventh.

Example:

As with triads, the dominant seventh may be shown by a Roman numeral or a guitar symbol.

OR   A7

V7

C7 The letter by itself stands for a major triad; the 7, when used with a letter, stands for a minor seventh.	**V7** The seventh can be major or minor; it is determined by the key signature. In a V7, the seventh is always minor.

5. When playing the following progressions, verbally spell each chord in root position, but play the closest position (as written).

a.

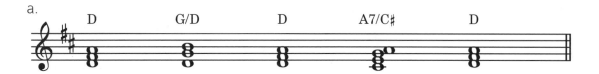

b.

c.

6. Review the pattern for major scales.

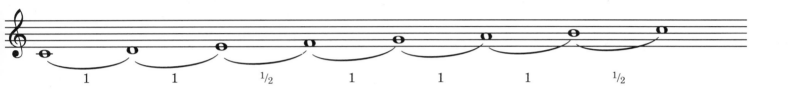

Build major scales on each of the following pitches.

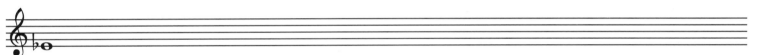

7. As with sharps, the flats in a key signature occur in a traditional order. Study each of the following major key signatures carefully, and then copy each in the space provided.

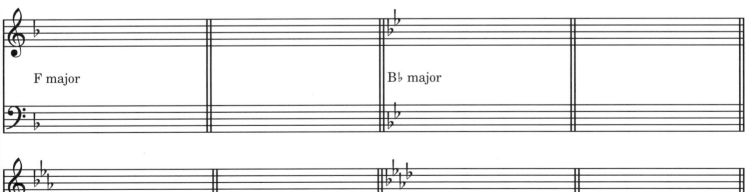

F major

B♭ major

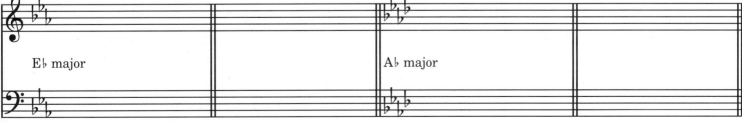

E♭ major

A♭ major

HARMONIZING

1. Play through Roman numeral chords in closest position before harmonizing.

FRANZ JOSEPH HAYDN
(1732–1809)

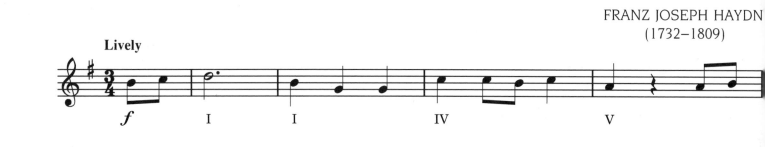

2. Play also in D major and G major.

American

3. Use closest position.

German

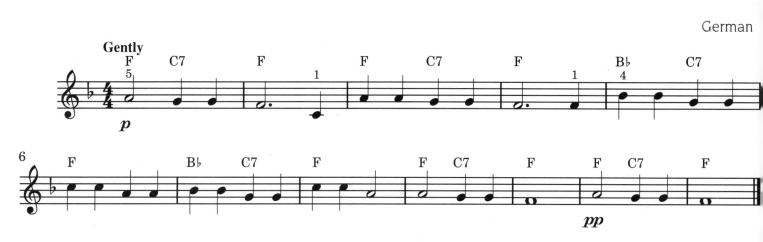

4. The first note of each measure of the chorus is given. Determine the rest by ear, and play as you sing.

Goodnight, Ladies

American

Good - night,   la - dies, _____   Good - night,   la - dies, _____

Good - night,   la - dies, _____   We're going   to   leave   you   now.

Mer-ri-ly we roll a-long,   Roll a-long, roll   a-long.   Mer-ri-ly we roll a-long,   O'er the deep blue sea.

READING

1. With hand away from keyboard, think:

- Interval
- Keyboard location
- Fingering

Then play.

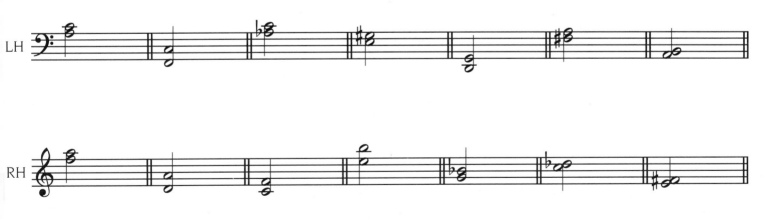

LH

RH

Play again, this time with the Cassette background.

14-2

2. Count two measures of pulses before playing each example with an upbeat.

a.
1 2 3 | 1 2

b.
1 & 2 & | 1 & 2

c.

3. Use "tabletop" practice to secure finger crossings in measures 13–16, then play as written.

Hopak

ALEXANDER GOEDICKE
(1877–1957)

simile*

*simile means to continue in a similar manner

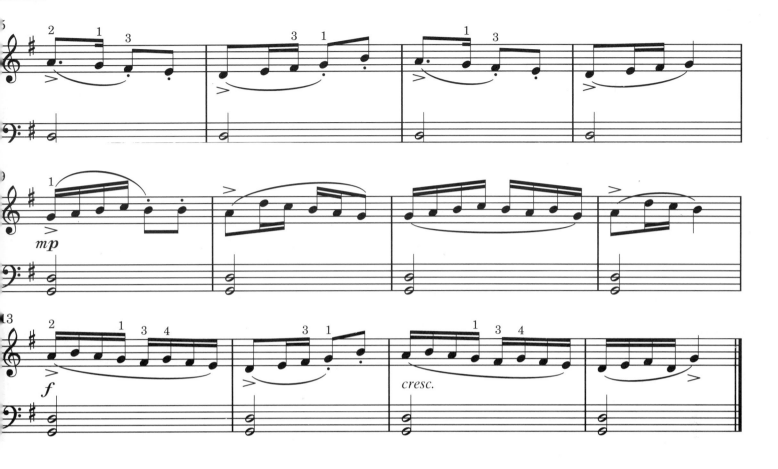

IMPROVISING

1. Create a "blues trio" in F:

14-3

- Part 1—melody based on the F blues pentascale

- Part 2—blues intervals that follow the I–IV–V pattern

I IV V

- Part 3—walking bass that follows the I–IV–V pattern

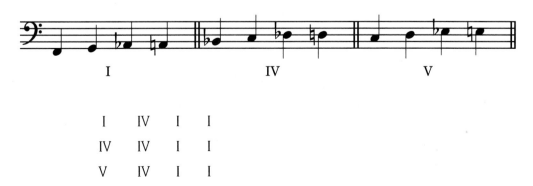

I IV V

I	IV	I	I
IV	IV	I	I
V	IV	I	I

The Cassette will provide a rhythm background. Play twice.

2. Improvise a right-hand melody to the rhythm of Hey, Ho! (p. 234). Use the following right-hand position. Next accompany with the ostinato shown.

RH Position

Ostinato

etc.

Now here is one traditional melody for Hey, Ho! Create your own left-hand ostinato using a low E and B.

Hey, Ho!

English

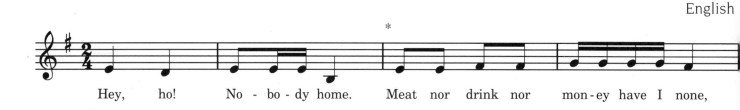

Hey,   ho!   No - bo - dy home.   Meat nor drink nor   mon-ey have I none,

Yet   I will be   mer - ry, mer - ry, mer - ry.   Hey,   ho!   No - bo - dy home.

Next, establish a low ostinato for two people to play. Divide the balance of the group into four parts and perform as a round with ostinato. For part 1, play where written; for other parts, select different keyboard ranges.

PERFORMANCE

1. *Hello, Ma Baby* may be performed in several different ways. Try the following combinations according to the needs of your class.

- As a six-part ensemble, each student playing only one part
- As a four-part ensemble, parts 2 and 3 combining into the Primo part and parts 4 and 5 into the Secondo part; parts 1 and 6 will remain single line parts
- As a duet, Primo and Secondo; parts 1 and 6 will be omitted
- A combination of two options with the change occurring at the repeat

Hello, Ma Baby

JOSEPH E. HOWARD
Arranged by Ann Collins

Today Is Blue

ARLETTA O'HEARN

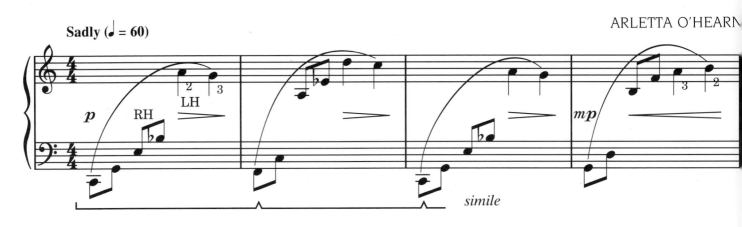

America, the Beautiful

SAMUEL A. WARD
Arranged by L.F.O.

Autumn Is Here

WILLIAM L. GILLOCK

Slowly, with a singing tone

*Pedal may be used.

All Through the Night

Welsh
Arranged by L.F.O.

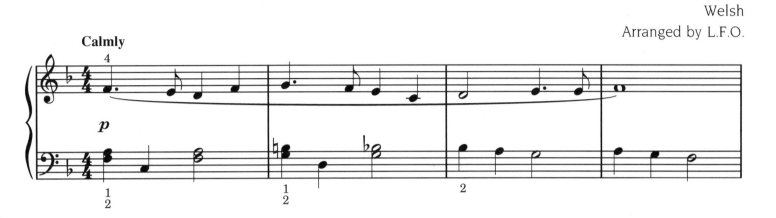

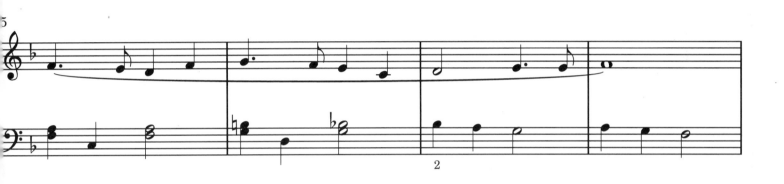

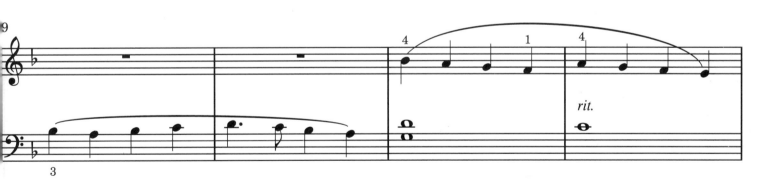

252

15.

Compound Meter/Key Triads

LISTENING

15-1

1. You will hear a musical example with six sections, each one announced with a number. Only three different musical ideas are used. The first section can be labeled A. If the second section sounds the same, it will also be labeled A; if different, it will be called B. Somewhere, a C will also occur. The resulting order of letters is an outline of the *form*. Listen once, straight through. Then listen again, this time listing letters for the six sections.

1. _____   4. _____

2. _____   5. _____

3. _____   6. _____

2. Find the first three keys of the D-major pentascale in your right hand. Your teacher will play four-measure phrases using these pitches. Play back after each four-measure phrase. Close your book!

Ear Investment No. 3

WOODY BUDNICK

3. You will hear three rhythm examples on the Cassette. Tap back after each example.

RHYTHM

1. In each of the rhythms below, the eighth note receives one pulse. Count aloud as you tap the rhythms for each.

a.

b.

c.

Compound Meter   Time signature having a triple pulse within each basic beat:

$$\mathbf{\frac{6}{8} \quad \frac{9}{8} \quad \frac{12}{8}}$$

2. Tap and chant the following "spoken ensemble."

Song of the Pop-Bottler

Poem by MORRIS BISHOP
Arranged by L.F.O.

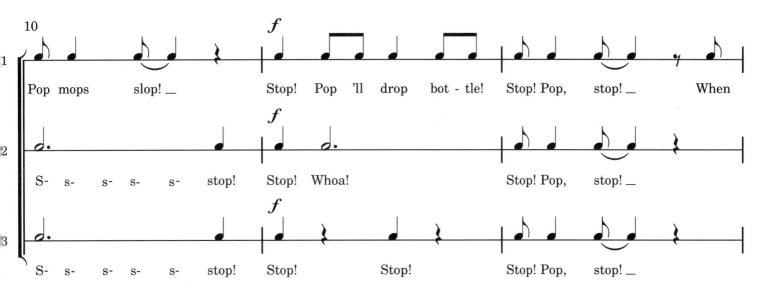

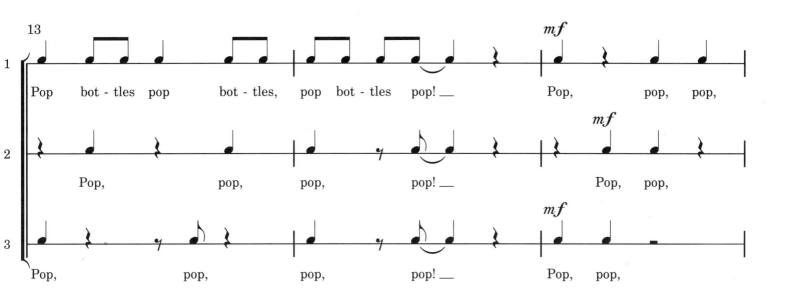

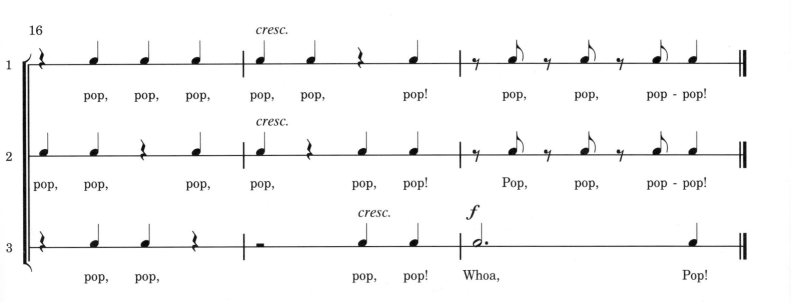

TECHNIQUE

1. The key of D-flat major contains five flats. The arrangement of the flats within the actual scale makes D-flat major one of the easiest scales to perform. To understand the grouping of fingerings, study the following example.

Play the two- and three-black-key groups, hands together, blocked.

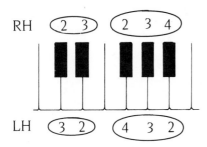

Play again, and this time use thumbs as pivots to move from one black-key group to the other (thumbs on F and thumbs on C). Block the D-flat major scale, hands together, two octaves up and down.

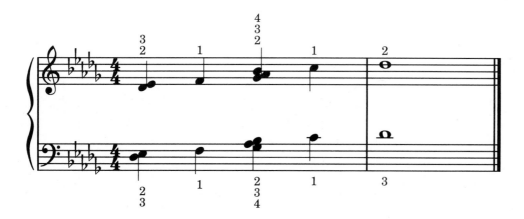

Now play the D-flat major scale as individual tones, hands together. Keep your fingers close to the keys, covering positions as shifts occur.

Transfer the same principle to G-flat major and B major.

THEORY

1. Play triads in the left hand on each tone of the C-major scale. Determine the quality of each triad (major, minor, diminished).

Play triads in the left hand built on each tone of the following major scales:

D   E   F   G   A

Play triads in the right hand built on each tone of the following major scales:

D   E   F   G   A

Play triads, hands together, as directed by the Cassette.

15-3

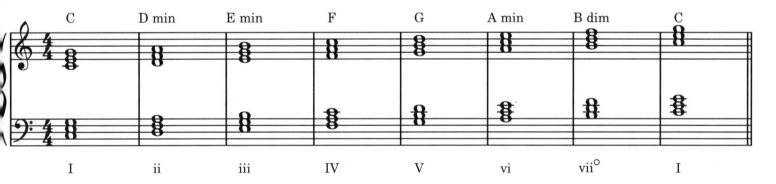

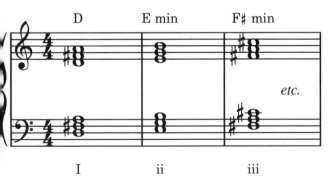

etc.

> **Relative Minor** Shares the key signature of the relative major.

2. All minor scales are derived from their relative majors and use the same key signatures. The *natural minor* scale can be observed within the major scale pattern, beginning on the sixth scale degree.

| **Natural Minor** Uses the key signature of the relative major |  |

Harmonic Minor Raises the 7th scale degree one half step

HARMONIZING

1. Harmonize the following melodies with the chords indicated. Accompaniment styles have been suggested.

a. Broken chord

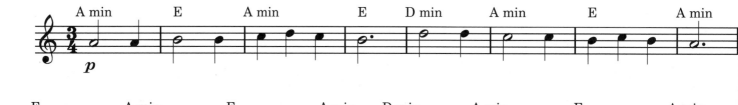

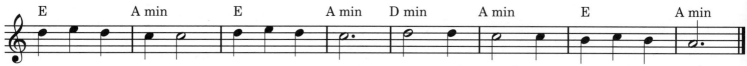

b. Blocked chord in closest position

Sometimes I Feel Like a Motherless Child

c. Broken chord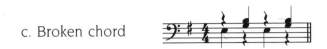

c.   Spiritual

Red River Valley

d. Root chord, fifth chord, as you sing

American

e. Blocked chords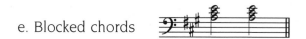

f. Two-handed "boom-chick-chick" as your teacher plays melody

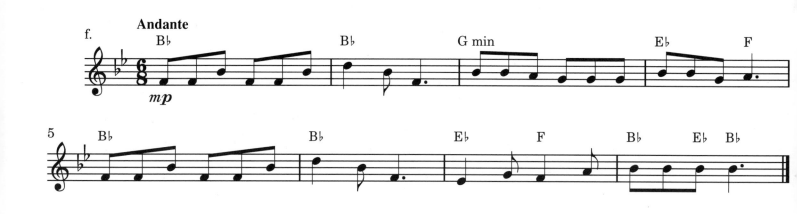

g. Broken chord

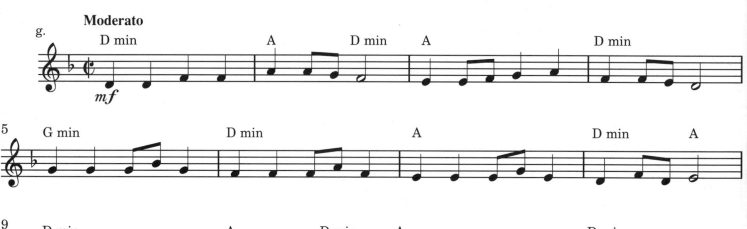

READING

1. Play these examples that use minor keys.

a.

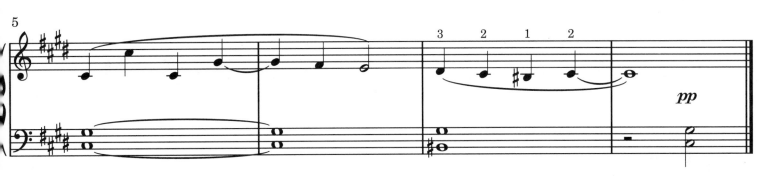

b.

c.

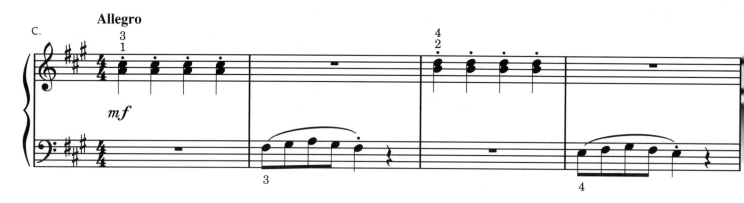

d.

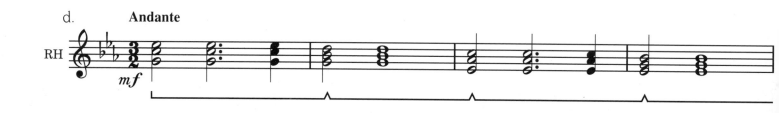

2. In what key is *Russian Song* written?

Russian Song

Russian
Arranged by L.F.O.

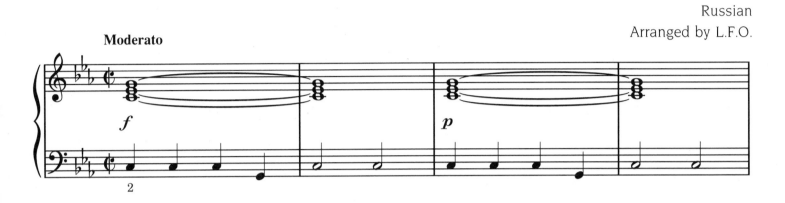

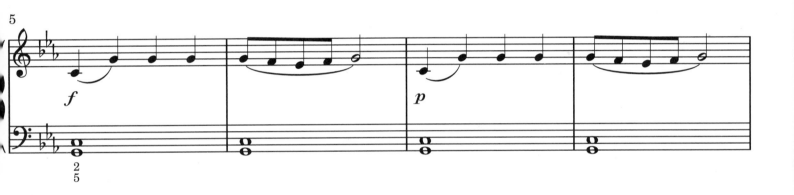

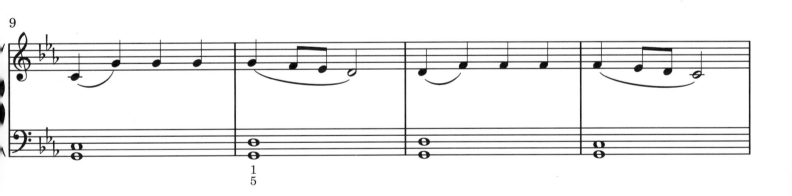

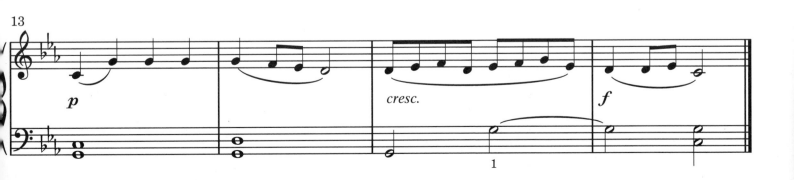

IMPROVISING

1. Play *Country Dance* six times, moving to the next part down each time (part 6 moves to part 1).

- First time, *p*
- Second time, *mp*
- Third time, *mf*
- Fourth time, *f*
- Fifth time, *p*
- Sixth time, *pp*

Country Dance

L.F.O.

Do-Mi-Fa-Fi

JUNE EDISON

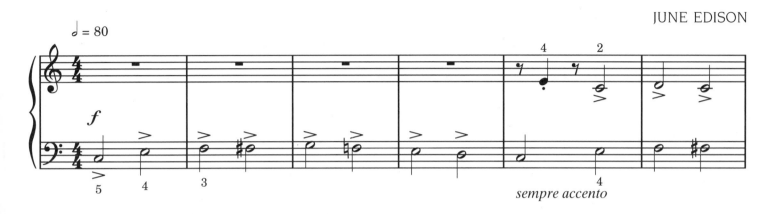

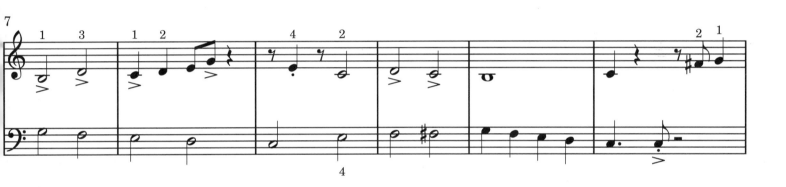

All Night, All Day

American
Arranged by L.F.O.

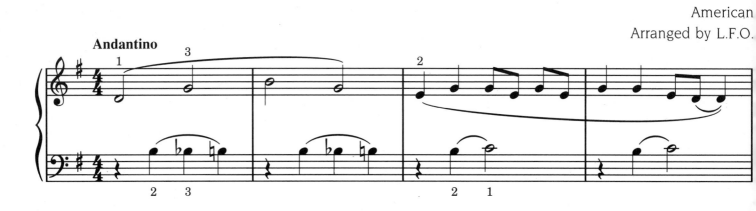

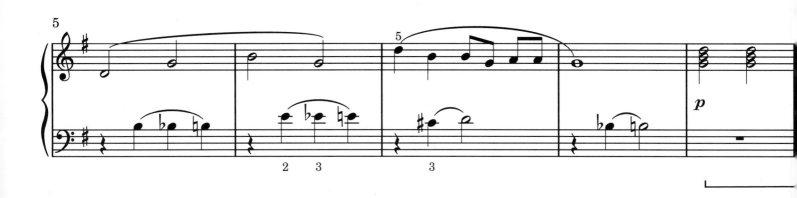

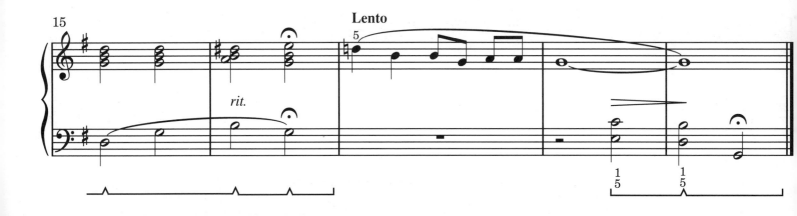

Triadique

L.F.O.

Prestissimo *

*Very fast.

O Sole Mio

EDUARDO DI CAPUA
Arranged by L.F.O.

Beautiful Dreamer

STEPHEN C. FOSTER
Arranged by L.F.O.

Variations on a Theme by Haydn

JOHANNES BRAHMS
(1833–1897)
Arranged by M. Hilley

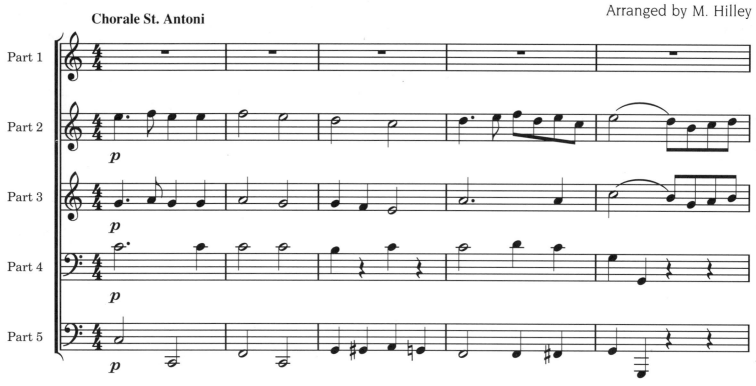

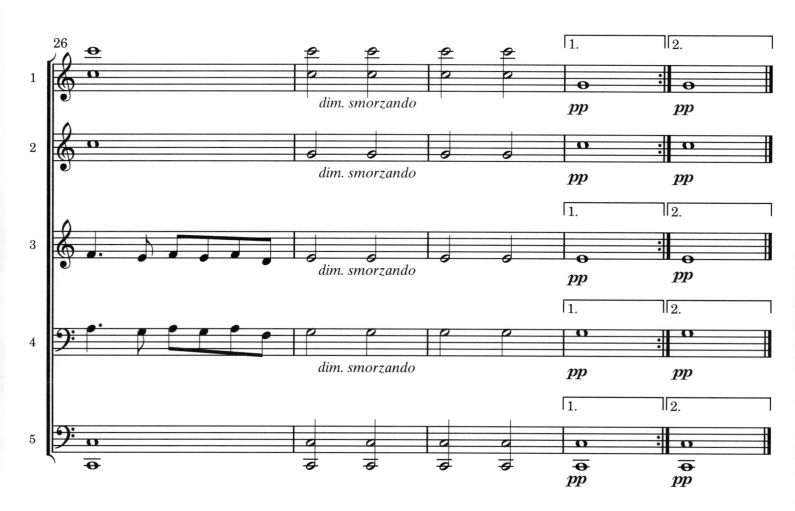

16.

Recap

Minuet in F

from L. Mozart's *Notebook*

LEOPOLD MOZART
(1719–1787)

Dziekuje,* Chopin

WOODY BUDNICK

*In Polish, "thank you"

Bay Breezes

RANDALL HARTSELL

*Possible on conventional keyboards

Sadness

DANIEL GOTTLOB TÜRK
(1756–1813)

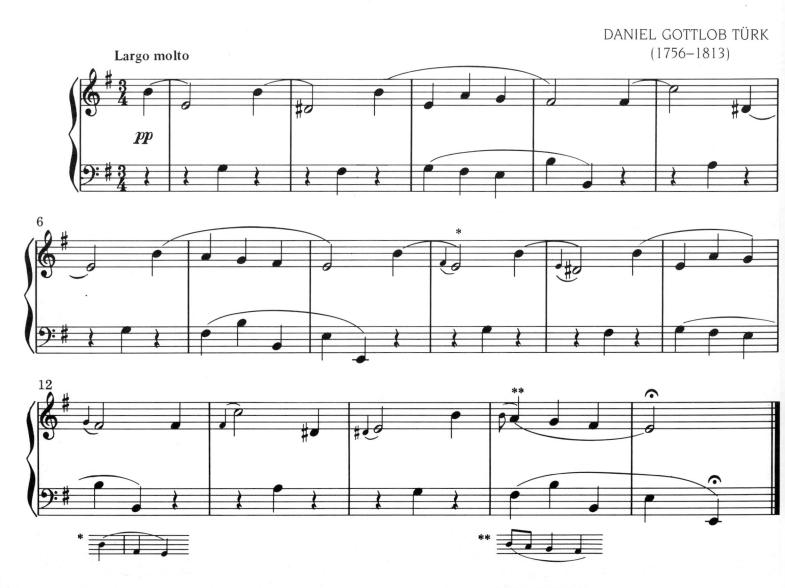

Home on the Range

American
Arranged by L.F.O.

Give My Regards to Broadway

GEORGE M. COHAN
(1878–1942)
Arranged by L.F.O

Etude in D

CORNELIUS GURLITT
(1829–1901)

Winter's Chocolatier

L.F.O.

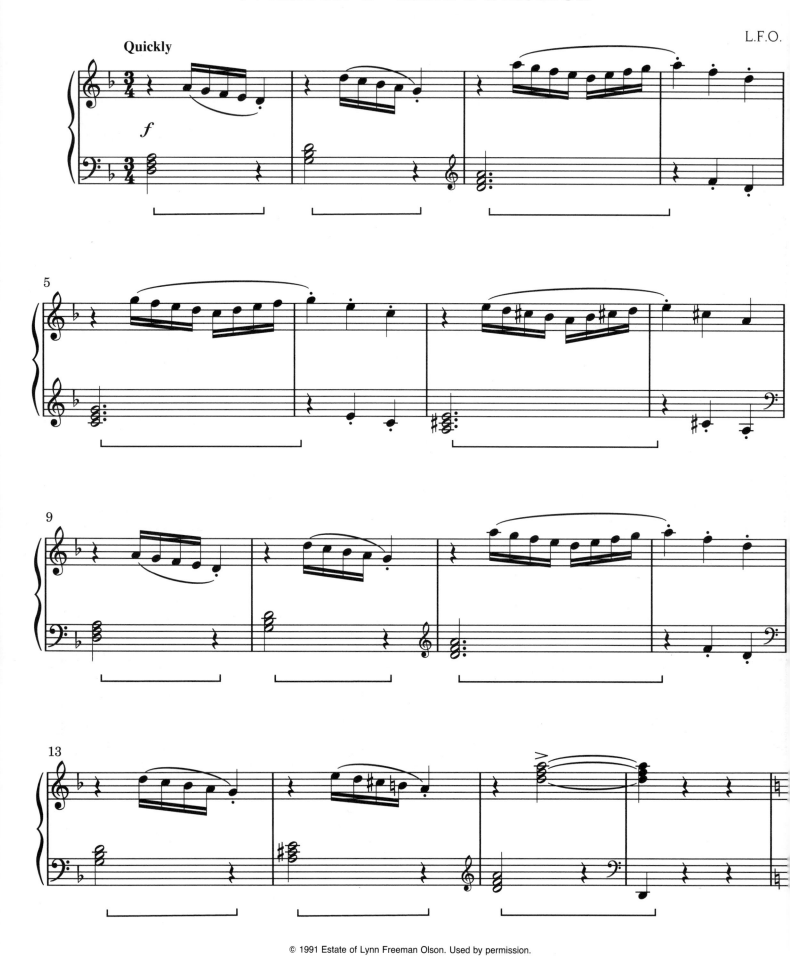

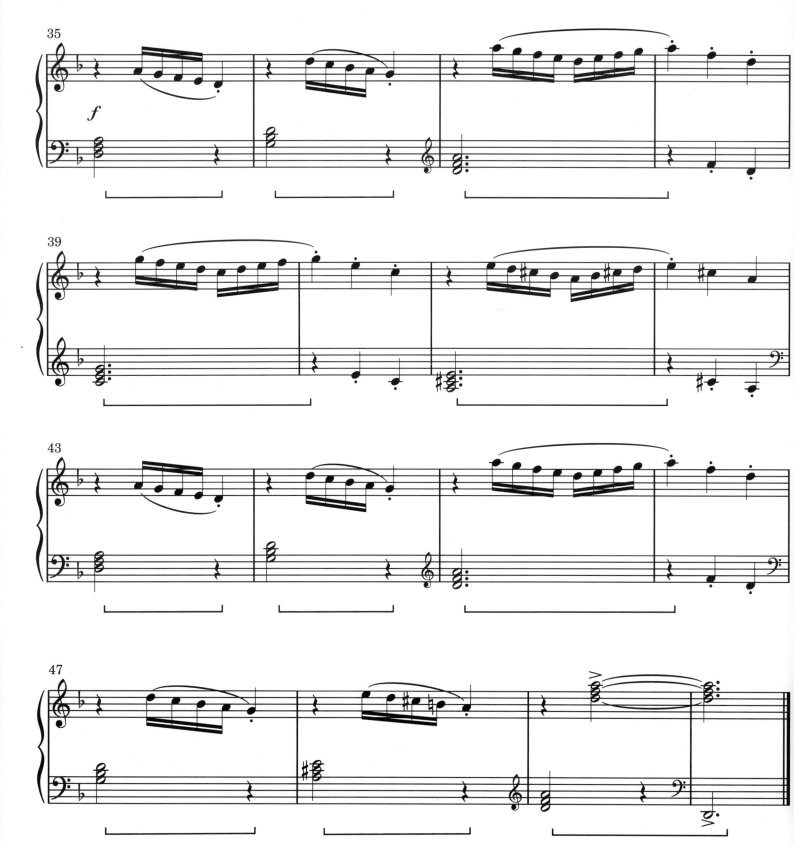

TERMINOLOGY REVIEW

Discuss the following musical terms.

- *Ritardando/accelerando/a tempo*
- Compound meter
- Inversion
- Major, minor, diminished, and augmented triads
- Relative minor
- Natural minor/harmonic minor
- Dominant seventh/C7/V7

WRITING REVIEW

1. Indicate the inversion for each of the following chords by using the appropriate guitar symbol.

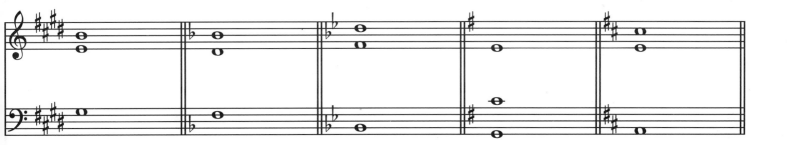

17.

Triplets/Primary Chords in Minor

LISTENING

1. Listen as your teacher plays the first phrase of the melody *Happy Birthday to You* in F major. The melody begins on the 5th scale tone. What is the meter?

   Listen again and play the phrase. Continue through the song.

2. Decide on another well-known melody or two you would like to play by ear. Proceed as in item 1 with your teacher's help as necessary.

3. Find the first three notes of the C-minor scale; start on middle C. Your teacher will play two-measure phrases using these notes. Listen carefully for syncopation. Play back after each two-measure phrase. Close your book!

Ear Investment No. 4

WOODY BUDNICK

Reprinted by permission of the composer.

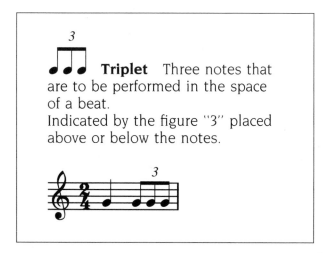

Triplet Three notes that are to be performed in the space of a beat.
Indicated by the figure "3" placed above or below the notes.

1. Tap the following rhythm exercises containing triplets. Count aloud!

a.

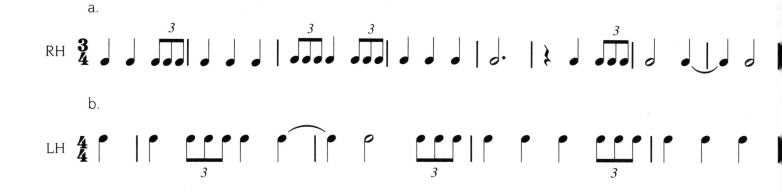

b.

2. Tap the following two-handed rhythms that use triplets.

a.

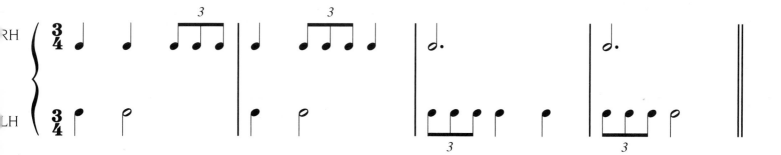

b.

c.

3. Tap the following two-hand rhythm exercises that use compound rhythm.

a.

b.

TECHNIQUE

1. Study the pattern of fingering for the white-key minor scales, two octaves.

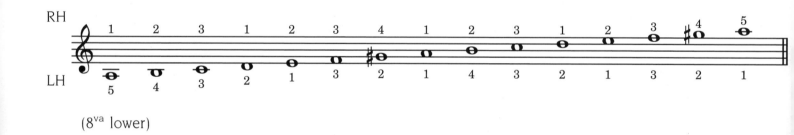

(8ᵛᵃ lower)

Does it look familiar?

Use this fingering in playing the following minor scales (natural and harmonic form), hands separately.

C   G   D   A   E

THEORY

1. Study the i, iv, and V chords as they are formed above the harmonic-minor scale.
   (Lower case Roman numerals are used for minor chords.)

i   iv   V

Play the following exercises using i, iv, and V triads in harmonic minor. Spell the next triad aloud during each measure of rest.

a.

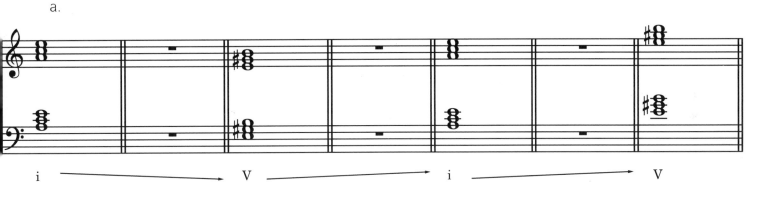

i ⟶ V ⟶ i ⟶ V

b.

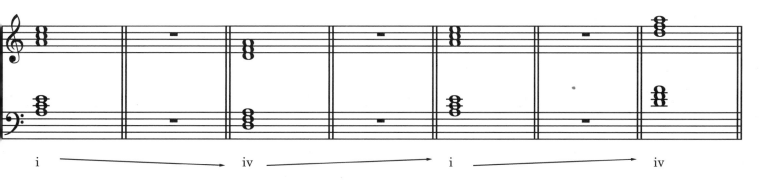

i ⟶ iv ⟶ i ⟶ iv

c.

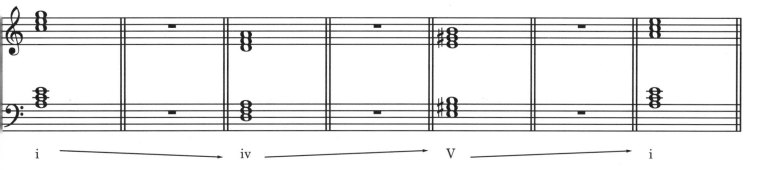

i ⟶ iv ⟶ V ⟶ i

Play the exercises again using these minor keys: C D E G.

2. There are many variations of writing guitar symbols for triads and seventh chords. The following table may help you to make up an accompaniment for a popular tune using the symbols shown in the particular piece of sheet music. The ability to figure out any chord lies in your ability to analyze the pattern of major and minor thirds used in the chord. Try playing these chords on other pitches and then "go for it!"

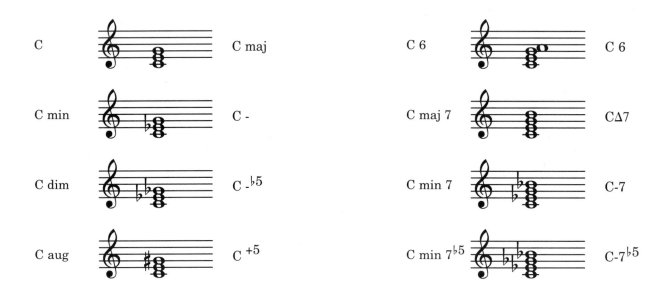

HARMONIZING

1. Harmonize the following melodies with the chords and accompanying suggestions indicated.

Clementine

a. Two handed "boom-chick-chick" as you sing

American

Scarborough Fair

b. Broken chord or strumming pattern as you sing

Wistfully

British

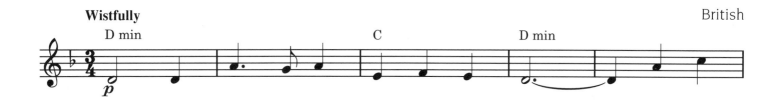

Keyboard style   A style of accompanying in which the melody and chords are in the right hand (three notes); root or indicated bass note in the left hand.

The melody note must stay in the highest sounding voice in the right hand.

Amazing Grace

c. Keyboard style

American

Canterbury

d. Blocked chords

British

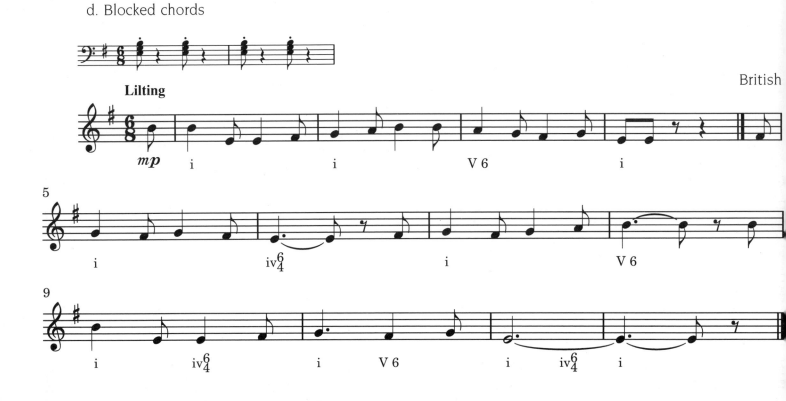

Lonesome Road

e. Two-handed broken chord as you sing

American

etc.

Hush, Little Baby

f. Complete in the style indicated

American

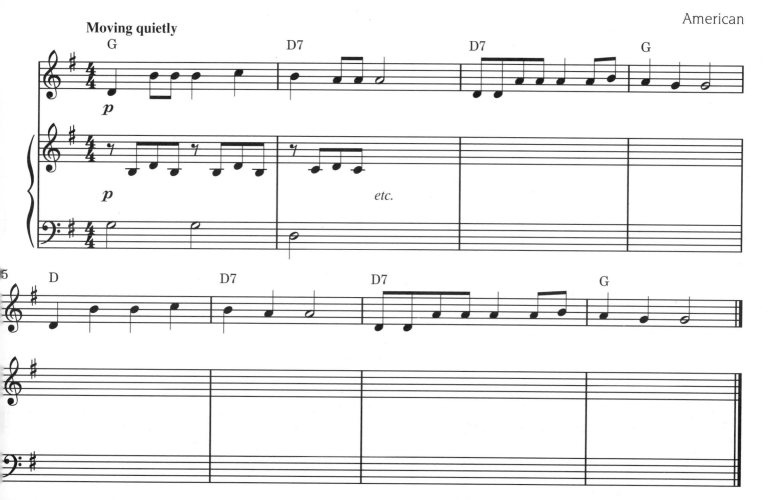

2. Determine an appropriate accompaniment style and perform.

When Johnny Comes Marching Home

American

He's Got the Whole World

Spiritual

Auld Lang Syne

Scottish

5

READING

Wayfarin' Stranger

American
Arranged by L.F.O.

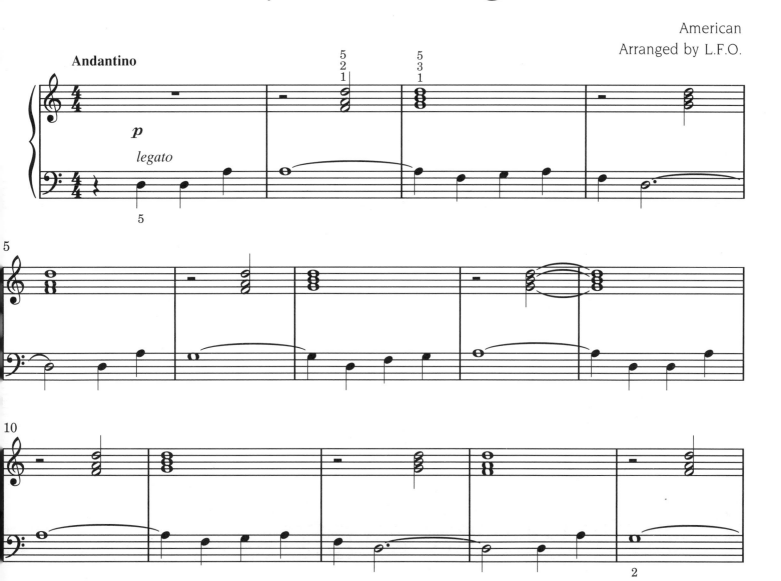

Wistful

WOODY BUDNICK

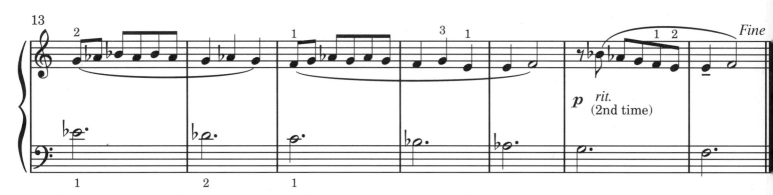

Streets of Laredo

American
Arranged by L.F.O.

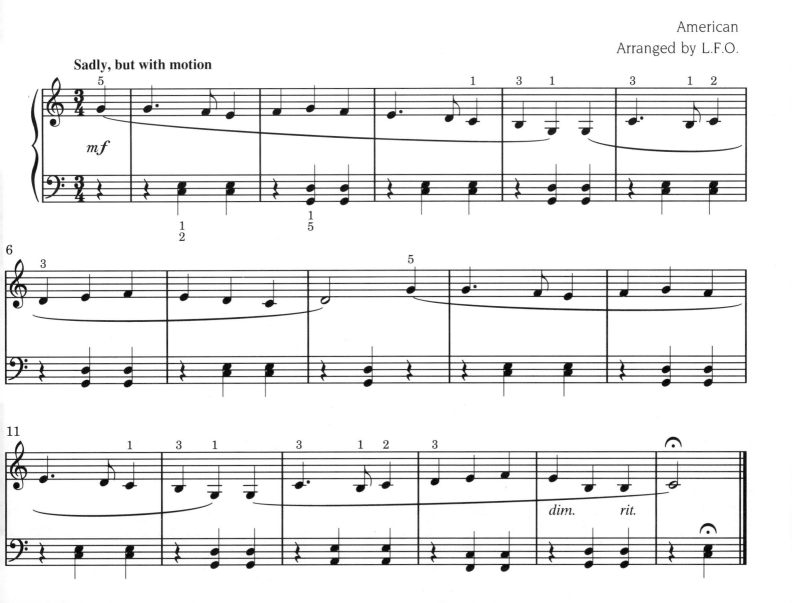

Minuet in B Flat

L.F.O.

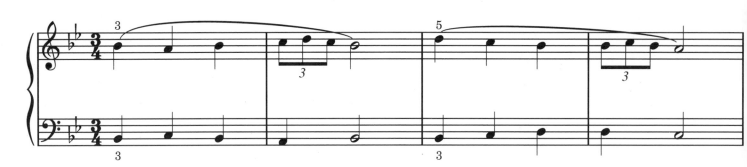

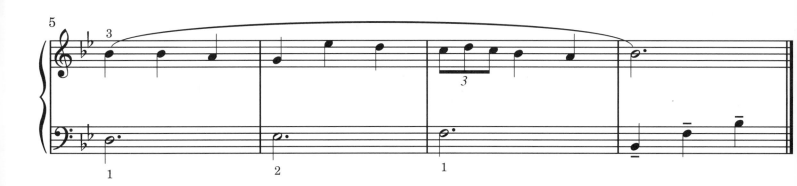

Berceuse

DANIEL GOTTLOB TÜRK
(1756–1813)

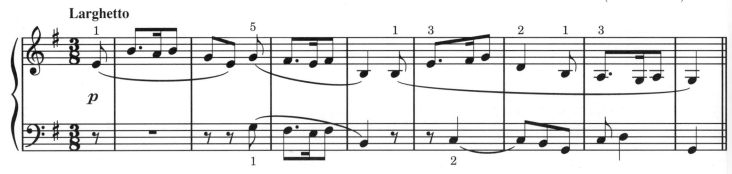

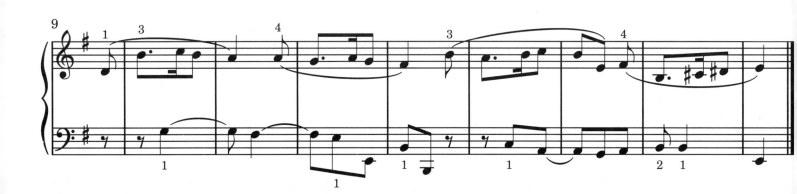

IMPROVISING

17-1

1. The melodic material found in most blues is based on the lyric, or the "sad tale of woe." Look closely at the verse written below and notice the repetition of the first and second set of four bars. The formula could be:

> State a problem (4 bars)
> Restate a problem (4 bars)
> Try to find a solution (4 bars)

Write two twelve-bar verses of your own to follow the verse shown. Improvise melodically as the Cassette provides a background for three choruses of blues.

> I hate to see,
> That evenin' sun go down.
>
> Oh, I hate to see,
> That evenin' sun go down.
>
> That man of mine,
> He done left this town.

PERFORMANCE

German Dance

LUDWIG van BEETHOVEN, WoO 42
(1770–1827)

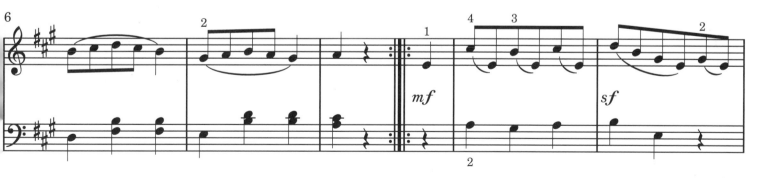

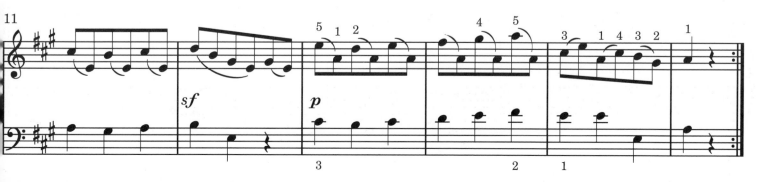

The Frog Level Concerto*

JOSEPH M. MARTIN

*Frog Level is a small town in North Carolina.

The rest of this page has been left blank to avoid difficult page turns.

Lazybones Blues

ATTICA AITKENS

Rhythm Machine

L.F.O.

Wishing

ROBERT D. VANDALL

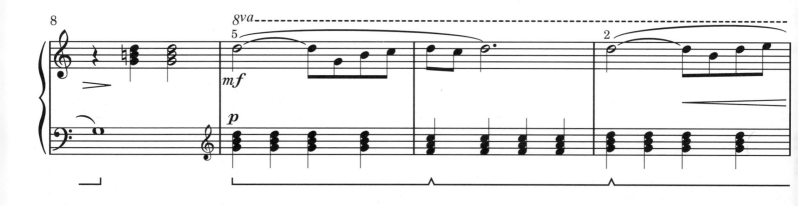

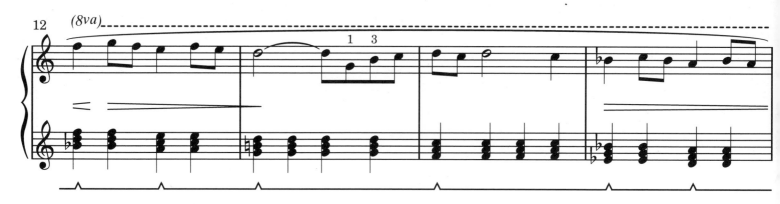

320

18.

Supplementary Repertoire

Musette

from J.S. Bach's *Notebook for Anna Magdalena Bach* (1725)

UNKNOWN

Yankee Doodle Boy

GEORGE M. COHA

Arranged by L.F.

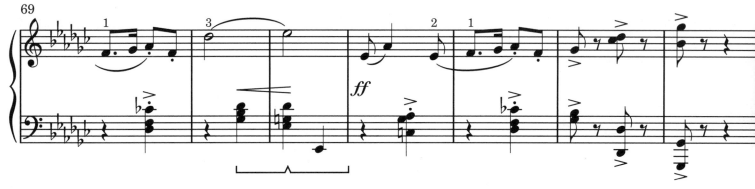

The rest of this page has been left blank to avoid difficult page turns.

18

Soldiers' March

ROBERT SCHUMANN, Op. 68, No. 2
(1810–1856)

Spurs

L.F.C

Moonlight

Up-stems RH
Down-stems LH

WILLIAM L. GILLOCK

Andante sostenuto (sustained)

Largo

ARCANGELO CORELL
(1653–1713)

p cantabile

Camptown Races

STEPHEN C. FOSTER
(1826–1864)

Arranged by Dorothy Bishop

Quickly

mf

mp   *mf*

18

Camptown ladies sing this song—
   Doo-dah! Doo-dah!
Camptown racetrack five miles long—
   Oh! Doo-dah day!

Came down there with my hat caved in—
   Doo-dah! Doo-dah!
Went back home with a pocket full of tin—
   Oh! Doo-dah day!

   Going to run all night!
   Going to run all day!

I'll bet my money on the bob-tail nag—
   Somebody bet on the bay.*

*First published in 1850.

Gypsy Dance

FRANZ JOSEPH HAYDN
(1732–1809)

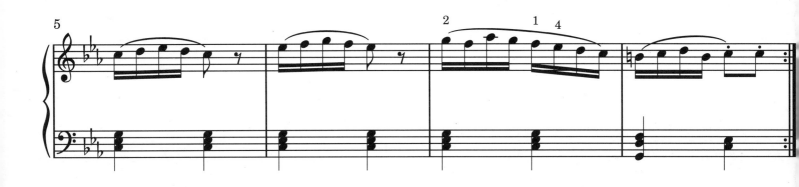

18

Hark! The Herald Angels Sing

FELIX MENDELSSOHN
(1809–1847)
Arranged by M. Hilley

In a stately manner

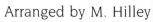

Silent Night

FRANZ GRÜBER
(1787–1863)
Arranged by M. Hilley

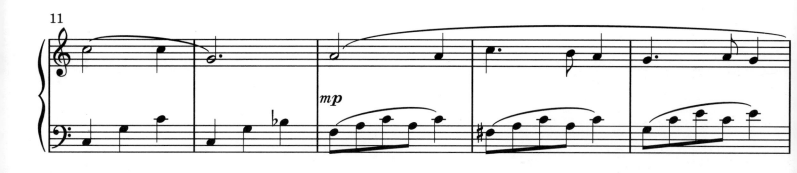

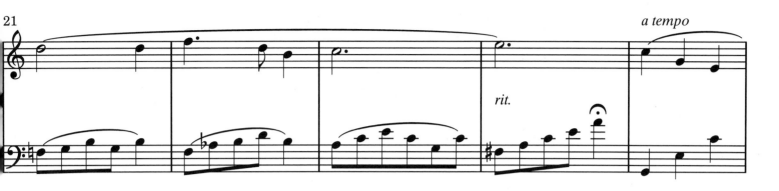

The rest of this page has been left blank to avoid difficult page turns.

O Little Town of Bethlehem

O little town of Bethlehem, How still we see thee lie!
Above thy deep and dreamless sleep, The silent stars go by;
Yet in thy dark streets shineth The everlasting Light;
The hopes and fears of all the years Are met in thee tonight.

LEWIS H. REDNER
(1830–1908)
Arranged by L.F.O

Appendix A—Major Keys

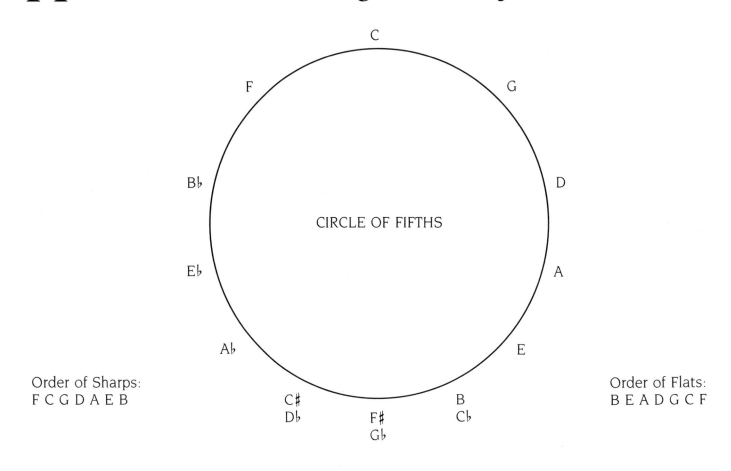

Order of Sharps:
F C G D A E B

CIRCLE OF FIFTHS

Order of Flats:
B E A D G C F

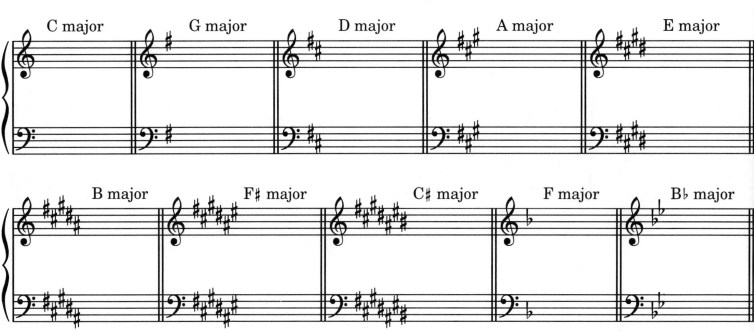

Appendix B—Major Scales

The following major scales use "black-key-group" fingering.

Db major

Gb major

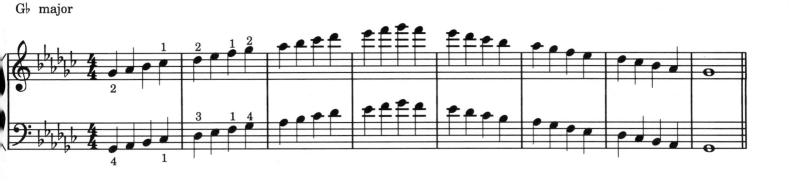

Cb major

Appendix B

The following enharmonic scales use the same fingerings as above.

C♯ major

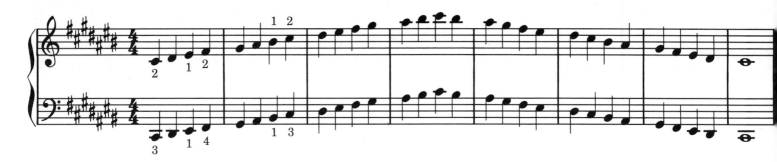

F♯ major

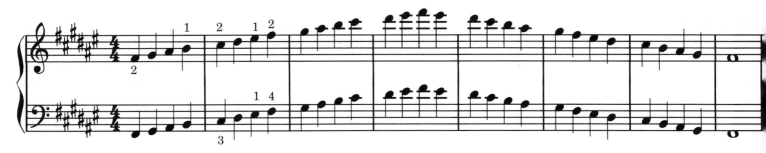

B major

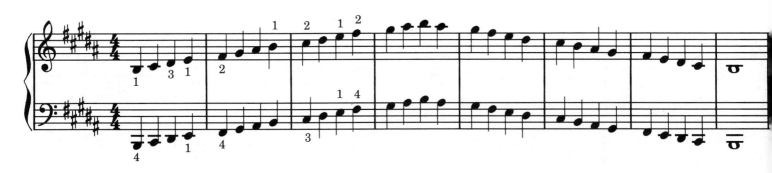

The following major scales use "C major" fingering.

C major

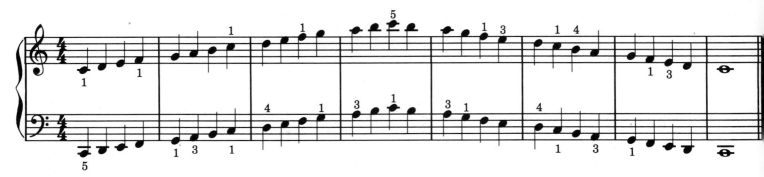

Appendix B

D major

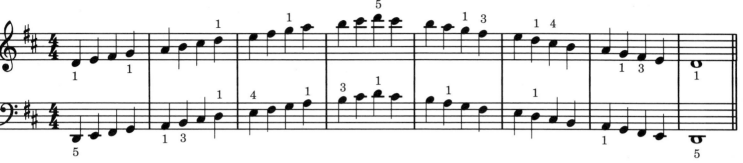

E major

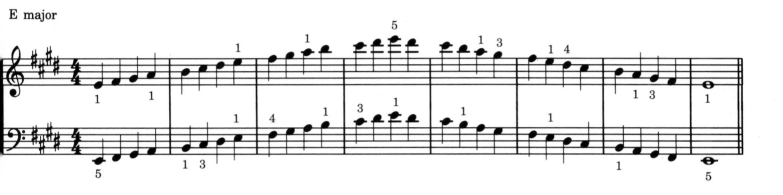

G major

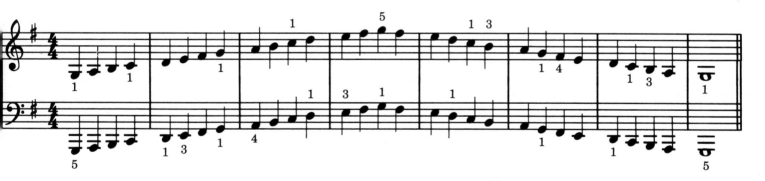

A major

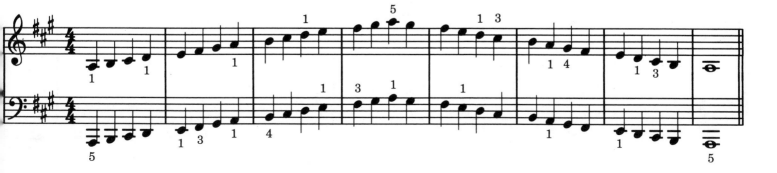

Appendix B

Ab major uses the same fingering "combination" as C major.

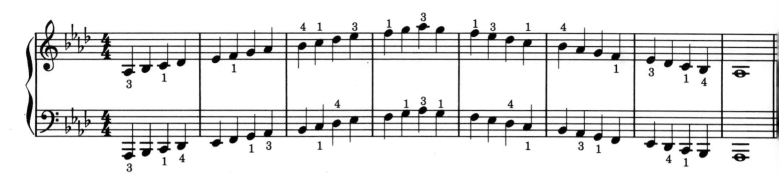

The following major scales are often called "the other majors"!

F major

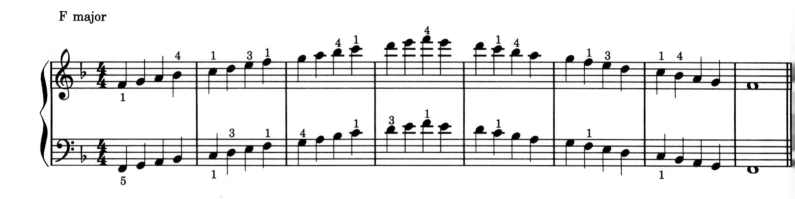

Bb major

Eb major

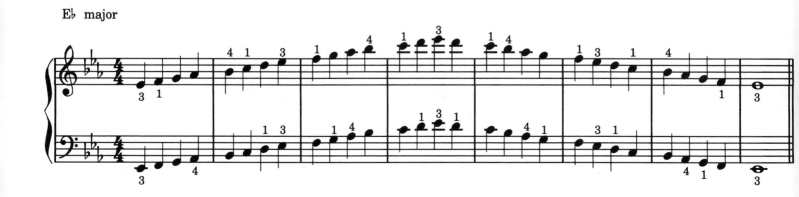

Appendix C—Minor Scales

These "harmonic" minor scales use C major fingering *or* the same fingering combinations as C major.

C minor

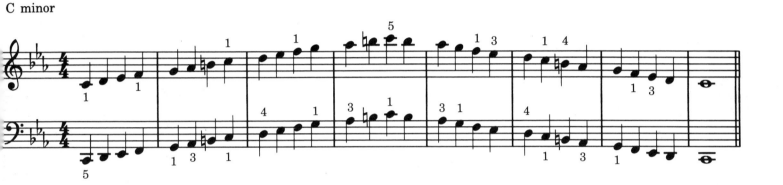

D minor

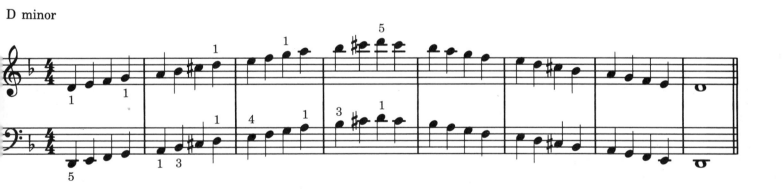

E minor

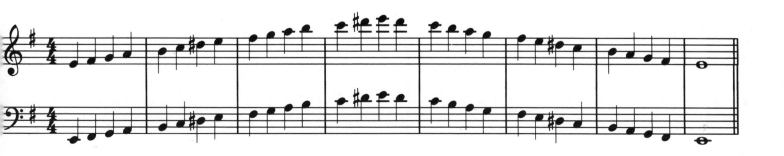

Appendix C

G minor

A minor

A♭ minor

F♯ minor

C♯ minor

The black-key-group minors use the same fingering combinations as the black-key-group majors.

B♭ minor

Appendix C

E♭ minor

G♯ minor

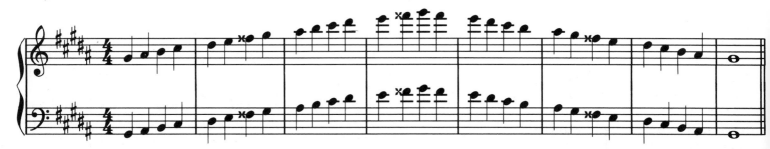

Use the same fingering as F major!

F minor

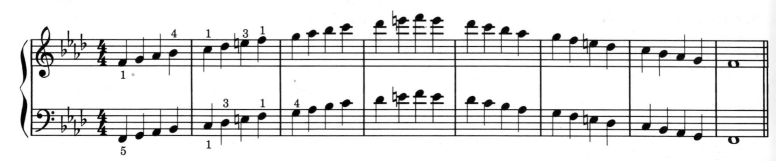

Glossary

a tempo   return to original tempo or previous tempo after such indications as rit. or accel.
accelerando (accel.)   becoming faster
accent (>)   sudden strong emphasis
Allegretto   a little less allegro
Allegro   bright, moderately fast
Andante   moderately walking
Andantino   a little faster than Andante

Cantabile   singing
chord inversion   root position rearranged
compound meter   time signature having a triple pulse within each basic pulse
crescendo (cresc., <)   to get gradually louder

decrescendo (decresc., >)   to get gradually softer
dominant   fifth tone of a scale
dominant seventh   chord built of fifth degree of scale; consists of dominant triad plus a minor seventh of root
downbeat   beginning of a measure
dynamics   degrees of loudness and softness in music; intensity

enharmonic   two names for one key

F Clef   used to identify notes on bass staff
fermata (⌒)   hold longer than the indicated note value
flat (♭)   lowers a note one half step; effect lasts through the measure
forte (*f*)   loud
fortissimo (*ff*)   very loud

G Clef   used to identify notes on treble staff
Grand Staff   usually right hand plays upper staff and left hand plays lower staff; combination of treble and bass staves

half step   from one key to the very next, black or white
harmonic intervals (blocked)   notes played simultaneously
harmonic minor   raises the 7th scale degree one half step

interval   distance from one key (or note) to another

key   a group of related tones named for their home tone (keynote, or tonic)

key signature   a list of the sharps or flats used in a key
keyboard style   a style of accompanying in which the melody and chords are in the right hands (3 notes); root or indicated bass note in the left

leading tone   the tone just preceding the tonic
legato   connected sound; special sign is not always necessary to show legato sound
ledger lines   used to indicate pitches above and below the five lines of the staff
Leggiero   lightly
Lento   quite slow

major pentascale   uses the following pattern of whole and half steps: 1   1   1/2   1
Marcato   with marked emphasis
measure   set of equal pulses marked off by barlines
melodic intervals (broken)   notes played one after the other
meter signature (time signature)   symbol used to indicate number of pulses contained in a measure; also indicates type of note value that will receive one pulse
mezzo forte (*mf*)   medium loud
mezzo piano (*mp*)   medium soft
Moderato   moderate tempo
music alphabet   seven letters, A B C D E F G, which are repeated over and over for full range of keyboard

natural (♮)   sign cancels the effect of a sharp or flat; effect lasts through the measure
natural minor   uses only the key signature of the relative major

ostinato   short pattern of sounds repeated continuously

pentascale   five-note scale using consecutive letter names
Pesante   heavily
phrase   musical "sentence" that may or may not be indicated by a curved line; may vary in length
pianissimo (*pp*)   very soft
piano (*p*)   soft

relative minor   shares the key signatures of the relative major
repeat sign   return to the beginning and play again, or return to the previous repeat sign and play again

Glossary

ritardando (rit.)   gradual slowing of tempo

root position   the name of the chord is the lowest sounding pitch

scale   individual pitches arranged in consecutive order

Scherzando   playfully

sharp (♯)   raises a note one half step; effect lasts throughthe measure

skip (3rd)   from one letter name over the adjacent letter name, up or down; two space notes or two line notes

slur   curved line above or below a group of notes to indicate that they are to be played in a connected manner

staccato   shortened sound; indicated by a dot above or below the notehead; to pull apart

staff   traditionally consists of five lines and four spaces

stem direction   upward—placed to right of note head; downward—placed to left of note head

step (2nd)   from one letter name to very next letter name, up or down; line to space or space to line

subdominant   fourth tone of a scale

syncopation   an emphasis on off-beats or weak beats

tie   curved line connecting two adjacent notes of same pitch; first note is played and held through value of second note

tonic   home tone or keynote

transposition   writing and/or performing music in a key other than the original key; think the new key and intervals

triad   the first, third and fifth notes of a pentascale; first tone is called "root"

triplet   three notes to be performed in the space of two; indicated by the figure "3" placed above or below the notes

upbeat   one or more sounds preceding a downbeat; last measure is usually shortened as a result

Vivace   lively, very fast

whole step   two half steps

Index of Titles